Stop Overthinking:

23 Techniques to Relieve Stress, Stop Negative Spirals, Declutter Your Mind, and Focus on the Present

by Nick Trenton

www.NickTrenton.com

Table of Contents

Chapter 1. Overthinking Isn't About Overthinking

Imagine a young man, James. James is kind, intelligent, and self-aware—perhaps a little *too* self-aware. James is always worried about something, and today, he's worried about a little health niggle that's caught his attention. He researches online and gets steadily more alarmed at the possibilities. Then he stops and checks himself: "I'm probably overthinking things," he thinks.

So he stops stressing about his health and starts stressing about his thoughts about his health. Maybe what he really needs is some therapy. But what kind? His thoughts run away with him, and soon he is inwardly debating his options for counseling, arguing with himself, putting himself on trial, defending himself, questioning himself, ruminating on endless memories, guesses, fears. He stops and checks himself. He wonders, "Is this what it's like to have anxiety? Is this a panic attack? Or maybe I have schizophrenia and don't even know it yet." He thinks that nobody else agonizes over nothing like he does, right? In fact, the moment he has that thought, his head is filled with seemingly millions of examples of all the times people have criticized him.

He then puts a magnifying lens on all his flaws and starts turning each of them over in his mind, wondering why he is the way he is, tortured by the fact that he can't seem to just "let it go." After an hour of this, he realizes with despair that he is no closer to making a decision about his health issue, and instantly feels depressed, sinking into a storm of negative self-talk where he tells himself over and over again that this always happens, that he never sorts himself out, that he's too neurotic . . .

Phew! It's hard to see how all of this torment and mental anguish started with nothing more than James noticing he had a weird-looking mole on his shoulder!

We all live in a highly strung, overstimulated, highly cerebral world. Overthinking puts our ordinary cognitive instincts in overdrive. Excessive thinking occurs when our thought processes are out of control, causing us distress. Endless analysis of life and of self is usually unwanted, unstoppable, and self-defeating. Ordinarily, our brains help us solve problems and understand things more clearly—but overthinking does the opposite.

Whether you call it worry, anxiety, stress, rumination, or even obsession, the quality that characterizes overthinking is that it feels awful, and it doesn't help us in any way. Classic overthinking often amplifies itself or goes round in circles forever, and thoughts seem intrusive.

Do you suffer from overthinking? Sometimes, it can be difficult to realize that this is in fact your problem, since overthinkers are pretty good at convincing themselves that their current worry is all-encompassing . . . until the next all-encompassing worry replaces it. Overthinking can certainly be a symptom and expression of other mental health conditions, such as generalized anxiety or depression, but the truth is that you can be an overthinker without these conditions.

Overthinking is excessively harmful mental activity, whether that activity is analyzing, judging, monitoring, evaluating, controlling, or worrying—or all of them, as in James's case!

You'll know that overthinking is a problem for you if:

- You are often conscious of your own thoughts moment to moment

- You engage in meta-thought, i.e. you think about your thoughts

- You try hard to control or steer your thoughts

- You are distressed by or dislike spontaneous thoughts and often feel that some thoughts are unwelcome

- Thinking for you often feels like a struggle between competing impulses

- You frequently question, doubt, analyze, or judge your thoughts

- In crises, you often turn to yourself and your thoughts as a source of the problem

- You are focused on understanding your thoughts and digging into the inner workings of your mind

- You have trouble making decisions and often doubt the choices you do make

- There are many things you're worried and concerned about

- You recognize yourself repeatedly engaging in negative thought patterns

- Sometimes, you feel like you can't help returning to a thought numerous times, even when it's in the past and nothing can be done about it anymore

You'll notice that some of the above are arguably good qualities—don't we all want to cultivate greater awareness and mindfulness? Isn't it good to question your knee-jerk reactions and ask yourself big questions so you can make better decisions? The gist of overthinking is in the name—it's when we think *over*, above and beyond what is beneficial for us.

Thinking is a marvelous gift. The ability to reflect, analyze, and interrogate even our own thought processes is arguably the single most defining characteristic of humankind, and the cause for many of our successes. Thought is not an enemy. Our brain is an extraordinarily helpful tool, but when we *over*think, we only undermine its power.

Causes for Mental Clutter and Agony

If the brain is such a wonderful thing and if thinking is so useful, then why is it so common and indeed so easy for people to get lost in overthinking? People over the ages (probably overthinkers) have proposed their theories: perhaps overthinking is a bad habit, or a personality trait, or a mental illness that can be medicated away. In fact, the reasons a person overthinks can often become a favorite topic of obsession for those who overthink. "*Why, why, why* am I like this?"

If you've picked up this book, it's likely that you have been distressed by how your own brain seems to run away with you. But there *are* solutions, and there are ways out of stress and ruination and into clearer, calmer waters. The first thing to note, however, is a big one: **the**

causes of overthinking are seldom the focus of overthinking. What does this mean? In James's example, his overthinking has nothing to do with the scary-looking mole on his back. It has nothing to do with choosing the right psychologist or what that person said to him twenty-three years ago or whether he should feel guilty for being a bad person.

All of these thoughts are the *result* of overthinking. When we are trapped in rumination, it can seem like the thoughts are the problems. We tell ourselves, "If I could just sort out this thing that's bugging me, I could relax and everything would be fine." But of course, even if that thing were resolved, another would quickly take its place. That's because it was never the cause of the overthinking, but the result.

Many overthinkers are at the mercy of an overactive brain precisely because they don't recognize what is actually happening. They are desperate to solve the "problem," not considering that their appraisal of what is a problem is in fact the problem. So, you might cling to some supposed solution and pour your energy into bringing that solution about, only to realize that you are precisely as stressed as you were to start with.

If we hope to successfully tackle overthinking, we need to take a step back rather than trying to work through the problem from inside our own rumination. And for the rest of this book, we're going to work on the assumption that when we are talking about overthinking, we are talking about *anxiety*. People can overthink without having a formally diagnosed anxiety disorder. But in the chapters that follow, we'll see anxiety as the root cause (the why) and overthinking as the effect (or the how). So then, where does anxiety come from?

Is it you?

Research into the causes of anxiety is ongoing. Competing theories suggest that it's a matter of personality, or a question of a biological predisposition—something you inherited from your equally anxious parents. Anxiety is often found with other disorders, both mental (like depression) and physical (like irritable bowel syndrome). But it's also been observed that certain groups—such as women—experience it more, and that elements like diet, stressful lifestyles, past trauma, and even culture have a part to play.

Marcus E. Raichle is a neuroscientist who coined the term "default mode network," which can be thought of as everything the brain does when it does nothing in particular. When no task dominates, the brain ends up mulling over its place in the world and processes and reprocesses social information and memories in the interests of increasing survival. In this way, the brain could be said to have evolved to survive, not to be happy.

The idea here is that mental "downtime" is used for additional processing—whether there's something to process or not. As physicist Michio Kaku said, "The human brain has one hundred billion neurons, each neuron connected to ten thousand other neurons. Sitting on your shoulders is the most complicated object in the known universe." And rumination is what happens when all that processing power has nothing better to do!

A 2010 paper published by Killingsworth and Gilbert titled "A wandering mind is an unhappy mind" found that the brain is ultimately spending as much time stewing over what is *not* happening as it is over what *is* happening. What's more, doing so generally leads to unhappiness. A 2008 paper by Broyd et. al. in the *Neuroscience Behavior Review* found that those suffering from anxiety and depression actually demonstrated greater default mode network (DMN) activation than others. Or should we interpret that to mean that those with greater DMN activity developed depression?

People are anxious about money, about work, about families and relationships, about growing older, or about stressful life events. But again, are these things causes of anxiety and overthinking, or are they the result? After all, many people experience enormous financial or family pressure and don't feel anxious or overthink, and others feel anxious when, from the outside, there doesn't appear to be anything causing the emotion.

To try to make sense of the abundant research out there, we'll take the approach that all of these theories have their place, and that anxiety is *multifactorial*—i.e. it results from a mix of different causes, which themselves have interesting ways of interacting. The first main reason you're anxious could be the nature part of the "nature vs. nurture" question. In other words, though it might not feel like it in the moment, a big cause of anxiety can come down to intrinsic factors within you as an individual.

Let's begin with a common explanation for anxiety: genetics. The truth is that no experts have been able to identify with absolute certainty a *single* genetic cause for anxiety. Researchers have, however, discovered a genetic component. Purves et. al. argued in a 2019 *Molecular Psychiatry* paper that chromosome 9 carries genes associated with the development of anxiety. But having these genes does not definitively mean you'll develop anxiety.

The paper goes on to explain that anxiety disorders have a heritability rate of twenty-six percent—what this means is that twenty-six percent of the variability in whether people develop anxiety disorders or not is explained by genetics. I'm sure you'll agree this is quite a small contribution—what about the other seventy-four percent? This comes down to your environment and things like your family history, past experiences, and current lifestyle. This kind of research can be difficult, because when you think about it, there are two ways to "inherit" anxiety from parents—one is genetically, but another is in the parenting we receive, our early formative experiences, and so on. In this way, it's difficult to pull apart genetic influencers from behavioral ones.

If you have a parent with an anxiety disorder, your chance of having one is greater—but this is still just a question of probability. There are no "anxiety genes" that destine you to a fixed fate you can never escape. There is even now evidence to suggest that as we get older and our environments change, the effects of our genes have even less influence over us. You can always learn to manage anxiety, work around it, and live well, if you're aware of any particular risk factors and predispositions.

The field of epigenetics now tells us that genes are only a part of the story. We are born with DNA that can be later altered through our life experiences and interactions with the environment. Certain genes can be activated or deactivated by molecular process, one of which is methylation. Epigenetic researchers are not only finding that life experiences can turn off genetic expression via methylation, but that this patten of methylation can in fact be passed down through generations.

Is overthinking genetic? Yes. But it's not *only* genetic. Life still weighs in on that seventy-four percent, which means that environment may play a bigger role. We can't do much about our genetics, but we can do a lot about everything else.

There are also other sources of anxiety within us besides genetics. Many of us have become habitual overthinkers because it gives us the illusion that we're doing something about the problem we're overthinking about. So, if James is worried about his health, it's natural that him overthinking endlessly about the various causes and solutions makes it seem like he's trying to get to the bottom of the issue. But the truth is that overthinking often doesn't lead anywhere, because the overthinker gets trapped in the cycle of analyzing, rejecting, and reconsidering different possibilities. It's like scratching an itch that just won't go away. You can scratch it to feel some momentary relief, but it won't make the itching stop despite how good scratching might feel.

Another reason it can be so hard to escape this vicious cycle is that the anxiety causing our overthinking works in clever and mischievous ways. It feeds on our worst fears. You might have noticed that your overthinking is exacerbated by some very specific triggers. This can be your insecurities about your personal capabilities, your relationships with certain people, your physical or mental health, etc. Simply trying to suppress your thoughts when they're running wild often results in the opposite outcome. You start thinking *even more* about the thing you were worried about. This might sound like a helpless situation, but later in this book, we'll discuss some techniques you can utilize to get out of this cycle.

Lastly, our daily habits can feed our anxieties and result in overthinking in subtle but significant ways. Seemingly innocuous habits like checking your social media often, not eating well or getting enough nutrition, not drinking enough water, having awkward sleep cycles, etc., can exacerbate our tendency to overthink things. Of all the factors we've mentioned so far, this one is by far the easiest to control. However, the next source of anxiety does not bend to our will as easily.

Is it your environment?

Your genetics might give you extremely fair skin that burns in the sun more than other people's, but whether you actually burn or not is not up to your genes to decide—it's up to the sun! In the same way, genes predispose us one way or another, but life itself plays the biggest role in developing and sustaining anxiety. In other words, genetic predisposition + stressful precipitating events = overthinking.

The classic view used to be that mental disorders lay purely within the person who had them— "chemical imbalances" in the brain, for example.

But we now understand that anxiety and related mental health conditions can definitely arise from, well, living in an extremely stressful world.

Stress is not a bad thing. "Eustress" or good stress is the kind of normal everyday pressure that inspires us, keeps us on our toes, and challenges us to be better. When stress is too great, however, it has the opposite effect and only works to deplete our psychological resources and leave us feeling unable to cope. On the other end of the spectrum, we can also be stressed by the complete lack of stimulation. Known as hypostress, this form of stress occurs when we aren't being challenged enough by our environment. This just goes to show that to flourish, we don't need a stress-free environment, we need one that's optimally suited to our needs.

Stress and anxiety are not the same thing. Psychologist Dr. Sarah Edelman explains that stress is something in the environment, an external pressure on us, whereas anxiety is our internal experience of this pressure. We all respond differently to the same stressful event because we all have different inner resources and thresholds, and our response can include other emotions (like anger or depression) and physical symptoms (like insomnia, digestive trouble, or lack of concentration).

Being alive is stressful. It's a normal part of our daily world to experience pressure, challenge, or discomfort. But if it's **persistent** and overwhelms our ability to cope and thrive, we can find ourselves exhausted, depressed, or with an anxiety disorder. The body's fight-or-flight response evolved to keep us safe—but we were never meant to *stay* in a heightened state of arousal indefinitely. If you heap chronic stress onto someone who already has a biological or psychological predisposition to overthinking, it's a recipe for burnout and overwhelm.

Work pressures, demanding children, an emotionally exhausting relationship, the never-ending stress of the twenty-four-hour news cycle, politics, climate change, the fact that your neighbor keeps making a noise upstairs, lack of sleep, too much junk food, that traumatic thing that happened to you last year, your low bank balance . . . It's no surprise many of us are completely overwhelmed.

Researcher Kenneth Kendler and his team found that both major depression and generalized anxiety disorder were strongly linked to traumatic life events in the previous month, such as bereavement, divorce, accidents, crime, or even things like experiencing poverty or racism. Several other studies (as early as Browne and Finkelhor, 1986) have found that one of the biggest predictors of mental disorders in adulthood was experiencing trauma, abuse, or neglect in childhood. In 2000, Christine Heim and colleagues suggested that sexual abuse in childhood had the effect of "sensitizing" women to stress in adulthood, meaning their physiological response to stress was actually heightened compared to other people.

When we think of environmental factors, we generally focus on the major events or parts of our experiences that contribute to overthinking. Many of these have been mentioned above, but there is also another sense in which environmental factors affect us. This is the immediate environments we spend substantial chunks of time in—our homes and offices/workspaces. How these spaces are composed and oriented can have a huge impact on how anxious we feel.

If you've ever heard, "Clean your room!" as advice for coping with stress, it's because of this very reason. Clutter, be it at home or work, is generally a significant cause of anxiety because it subconsciously acts as a reflection of yourself. Things like the quality of lighting, the smells and noises you're exposed to, the colors of the walls, and the people occupying these spaces with you can all cause or reduce anxiety and stress levels depending on how they're managed. You might be surprised at how much of an impact good lighting, pleasant aromas, and walls with calming colors have on your anxiety levels.

So, it is not just the genetic component that is responsible—life events and environmental stressors can make us more vulnerable to experiencing anxiety. To return to our earlier example, even if somebody had genes for dark, sun-resilient skin, if they're repeatedly exposed to harsh sun, they will nevertheless get sunburnt eventually.

To carry our metaphor just a little bit further, imagine again the person with pale and burn-prone skin. They may have been cursed with "sunburn genes," but they can also make conscious choices about their behavior (i.e., slather in SPF 50). In this way, they can deliberately choose to moderate the effects of the environment and take charge of their lives. This brings us to another, third aspect of the development of stress: our own behavior and attitudes.

The secret ingredient: our mental models

The nature vs. nurture debate has actually been resolved: it isn't either, but both—specifically, it's both together. Whether we experience anxiety comes down to the *relationship* between:

- Our unique genetic and biological characteristics and susceptibilities, and

- The events, pressures, and conditions we find in the external environment.

But we can all differ in how willing we are to examine this relationship, to understand it, and to take conscious control of it.

One final and powerful determiner of whether we experience anxiety or not is our unique cognitive style, our mental frames, and the behavior that these inspire in us. In picking up this book, for example, you've engaged with an influence on your life that is not strictly nature or nurture.

At the interface between nature and nurture is the story we tell about our lives, the way we make sense of things, our inner dialogue, and our sense of our own identity. The old saying goes, "It's not the load, but how you carry it." Whether you feel an event as stressful and overwhelming comes down to how you interpret and understand that event, as well as how you actively engage with it, i.e., what choices you make.

Two people can have vastly different appraisals of the same scenario—it is the appraisal that causes their experience, and not the scenario. Some appraisals of life simply lead to more stressful outcomes. If you're the kind of person who, for example, has an external locus of control (i.e., you don't see your life as really under your control, but influenced by luck, randomness, or other people), then you may see a certain new situation as a threat rather than an exciting challenge. And once you've told yourself it's a threat, you will behave as if it is—and get anxious.

Consider this: Siamese cats possess genes that give the coat its characteristic coloring. The genes, however, are not set in stone, but rather express themselves conditionally in relation to the environment because they are temperature-sensitive. They are "switched on" in colder areas of the body (the brown tail tip, nose, ears, and feet) and turned off in warmer areas. If you raise a Siamese kitten in a very cool climate, it will be darker brown. In a warmer climate, it will look lighter. Thus, two cats with the same genetic makeup end up with a different phenotype, i.e., physiological expression of those genes.

If a Siamese cat breeder decided to relocate their cats to a warmer climate because they wanted lighter-colored coats, we could say that the resulting color is neither purely down to genes nor down to environment. In fact, the color isn't even a result of the interaction between the two, but of some third variable: the breeder's awareness of how color works in Siamese cats, and their deliberate and purposeful action to get the outcome they desire.

Your perceptions, perspectives, sense of self, worldview, and cognitive models all go toward your interpretation of neutral events. We respond not to stress but to our perception of stress. And these perceptions are then made real in the world through action, which can ultimately reinforce those attitudes and worldviews.

In the chapters that follow, you won't find advice on how to change your genetics (impossible) or how to get rid of stress in the environment (slightly more possible, but only slightly). Rather, we'll be focusing on all the things you are empowered to do right now to change your outlook to better manage anxiety and overthinking.

People who overthink often have genetic and environmental "reasons" for their overthinking, but in the end, it's their unique evaluation that brings everything together in a particularly stressful way. What are your beliefs about your innate strengths and skills when it comes to resisting stress? How do you view the world and the challenges in it, and how much say do you have in how it all unfolds? What are your daily habits like? Is your self-esteem in good order? What about your boundaries? These are all the things that we *can* change.

In the remainder of this book, we're going to be looking at practical, concrete examples of how to incorporate things like cognitive behavioral therapy into your own life. With the right techniques, we can reframe our perspective and change our behavior, stopping us from overthinking and putting our brains to good use instead. We'll look at ways of strengthening your sense of control and empowerment, of generating hope and excitement rather than fear, of taking control of stress and steering your life, rather than feeling like it's steering you.

Before we dive in with techniques, let's consider what's at stake if we *don't* act in this way, and take our well-being into our own hands.

Consequences of Overthinking

Do you remember James from earlier in the chapter? We took a peek into his brain for just an hour or two, but imagine being James twenty-four-seven with a brain that seemingly never switched off. Perhaps you already know what this feels like. Yet most people don't think of worry and overthinking as innately harmful—it's just thoughts, right?

Wrong—*anxiety is a physiological, mental, psychological, social, and even spiritual phenomenon.* There is no aspect of life that anxious overthinking doesn't impact. When you perceive a threat, your HPA axis (hypothalamus, pituitary, adrenals) is stimulated. Your brain triggers a cascade of neurotransmitters and hormones in the body, which then have physical effects—this is the classic fight-or-flight response to prepare the body to survive the perceived threat.

Karin et. al. (2020) have published a paper outlining how the HPA system, when dysregulated, can form the bedrock of several related psychiatric conditions. Also, that's without mentioning the direct physiological effects of prolonged stress. From a systems standpoint, stress is a complex phenomenon that encompasses everything from the health and function of our endocrine glands and organs, to our adaptive behaviors, to our subjective experiences of our mood, and to the broader world we're a part of.

For James, the irony is that worrying about his health is literally harming his health. By cultivating a near-constant condition of stress and hyper-arousal, James ends up in a chronic, low-grade state of what is basically fear. The mole turns out to be nothing, but the low-grade fear that came with it quietly caused a host of other genuine issues: poor sleep, lack of concentration, a weakened immune system, etc.

So, it's not "all in your head"—it's all in your body, all in your behavior, and all in your world!

Physical effects, both long and short term, include:

Racing heart, headache, nausea, muscle tension, fatigue, dry mouth, dizzy feelings, increase in breathing rate, aching muscles, trembling and twitching, sweating, disturbed digestion, immune system suppression, and memory issues. Your body was designed to endure *brief* moments of acute stress, but chronic stress (stress that is ongoing) can start to cause chronic health conditions like cardiovascular disease, insomnia, hormonal dysregulation, and so on. If the ordinary physical experience of stress is prolonged, the physical effects can have consequences in the rest of your life.

Mental and psychological effects include:

Exhaustion and fatigue, feeling on edge, nervousness, irritability, inability to concentrate, lack of motivation, changes to libido and appetite, nightmares, depression, feeling out of control, apathy, and so on. Stress can reinforce negative thinking patterns and harmful self-talk, lower our confidence, and kill our motivation.

More alarming than this, overthinking can completely warp your perception of events in time, shaping your personality in ways that mean you are more risk averse, more negatively focused, and less resilient. When you're constantly tuned into Stress FM, you are not actually consciously aware and available in the present moment to experience life as it is. You miss out on countless potential feelings of joy, gratitude, connection, and creativity because of your relentless focus on what could go wrong or what has gone wrong.

This means you're less likely to recognize creative solutions to problems, see new opportunities and capitalize on them, or truly appreciate all the things that are going right for you. If you are constantly in a low-level state of fear and worry, every new encounter is going to be interpreted through that filter, and interpreted not for what it is but for what you're worried it could be.

Broader social and environmental effects include:

Damage to close relationships, poor performance at work, impatience and irritability with others, retreating socially, and engaging in addictive or harmful behaviors. A person who is constantly stressed and anxious starts to lose all meaning and joy in life, stops making plans, cannot act with charity or compassion to others, and loses their passion for life. There is very little spontaneity, humor, or irreverence when someone's mind is too busy catastrophizing, right?

As you can imagine, the physical, mental, and environmental aspects all interact to create one unified experience of overthinking and anxiety. For example, if you overthink consistently, your body will be flooded with cortisol and other stress hormones. This can leave you on edge, and in fact cause you to overthink even more, adding to the stress, changing the way you feel about yourself and your life. You might then make bad choices for yourself (staying up late, eating bad food, shutting people out), which reinforce the stress cycle you're in. You may perform worse at work, procrastinating and inevitably giving yourself more to worry about, and so on.

Environmental stress and pressure are neutral—they are not a problem until we pass them through our mental models and decide they are. When we ruminate and overthink, we can turn ordinary life stress into something overwhelming and negative. When we overthink, we get stuck in anxiety spirals, reinforcing a bad habit that has devastating effects on every area of our life, mind, body, and soul.

If overthinking has been a lifelong habit, you may have come to believe that it's basically a part of your personality. But take heart—change is possible, and it all starts with becoming aware of the role that overthinking is actually playing in your life. Overthinkers have an advantage over others: they are usually intelligent, aware, and able to take beneficial action for themselves—if only they are able to acknowledge that overthinking is not working for them anymore.

We all have different predispositions and degrees of resilience. We all have different exposure to stress in the environment. But the area we have the most control over is how we evaluate our experiences and move forward. Overthinking is not a natural state and is not necessary. It is a destructive behavior we can actively choose to stop if we want to. Stress is a fact of life, but overthinking is optional! With practice, anyone can retrain their brain to work on their side, to see things differently, and to resist the corrosion of constant anxiety and stress.

Takeaways

- What exactly is overthinking? Overthinking is when you excessively analyze, evaluate, ruminate, and worry about certain things to a point where it starts affecting your mental health because you simply can't stop.

- There are two main sources of anxiety that lead to overthinking. The first one is ourselves. Unfortunately, some of us are just genetically predisposed to being more anxious than others. However, genetics may not be the only factor. We might become habitual overthinkers because it makes us feel like we're somehow tackling the problem we're overthinking about. Because the overthinking never ends, this doesn't happen, but we still feel like we're making some progress. This turns into a vicious cycle that can be hard to escape.

- Another cause of anxiety is our environment. There are two aspects to this. First, we need to consider our immediate environments where we spend the most time, like our home and office. The way these spaces have been designed can have a huge impact on our anxiety levels. If they're cluttered, dimly lit, and noisy, it's going to make us more anxious. The second aspect is the broader experience we have in our socio-cultural setting through our interactions with the world. Something like experiencing racism or sexism might make us stressed and result in heightened anxiety.

- There are many negative consequences to overthinking. These include physical, mental, and even social harms that can become long-term issues. Some examples are racing heart, dizziness, feelings of fatigue, irritability, nervousness, headaches, muscle tension, etc.

Chapter 2. The De-Stress Formula and Then Some

So, we've painted a picture of what overthinking is, what's typically behind it, and how it can undermine our sense of wellbeing in life. We've also seen that the key to taking charge is to change our mental models and the way we think about the world. We need to de-stress!

Let's take a look at Angie, who is a professional stress pot and an Olympic-level worrier. Angie already *knows* that she overthinks and stresses too much about basically everything—you would have to be blind to not know this about her. Her problem is what to do about it.

"Just relax," people tell her. "Take a break."

Unsurprisingly, this not-too-specific advice achieves precisely nothing. Angie ends up booking complicated long-haul holidays that end up stressing her out even more, or forcing herself to pretend that she is enjoying a "pampering" spa break. As she sits in the silence in the massage room, all she can think about is every bit of stress waiting for her just as soon as she is finished and goes home.

Angie's problem is that she has no idea what "de-stressing" actually means or how to do it. She is told to "take your mind off things" and assumes that to relax, she needs to do less of what she's doing. But the irony is that the more she tries to turn her mind away from the things it's worrying about, the more determined it seems to focus on them, and the more she tries to do "nothing," the more impossible it seems!

This is why this chapter will not simply be more of the same advice, or a list of good reasons to take up meditation. For overthinkers, the ordinary de-stressing advice is usually not enough. In some cases, like for Angie, it makes things worse. Instead, we need to:

- gain conscious awareness of our thought process,

- be proactive about stress management, and

- learn real techniques to ground and focus our thoughts.

Our main goal in de-stressing is to pinpoint exactly what is going on in our heads when we overthink. It's about identifying the triggers that set us off as well as the effects of that overthinking once it begins. When we can see the process clearly, we can then begin to take informed action. But the necessary starting point? Awareness.

In this chapter, we'll begin with the basics of overcoming overthinking and managing your stress levels, but in each case, what is most important is that we maintain an *awareness* of ourselves. Awareness is not rumination, though: when we are aware, we simply turn our attention to both our inner and outer experience, without judgment and without clinging or resisting. In fact, one of the best skills an overthinker can develop is to distinguish between awareness and anxiety—the first is neutral, comfortable, and still. The second is tinged with emotion and tends to get carried away with itself. For overthinkers, we tend to go into anxiety when simple awareness is all that's called for.

Take Angie, for example. Everyone is always advising her to "stop overthinking things." When she ruminates, she does indeed feel bad, so she naturally assumes that . . . she just shouldn't think at all. As a result, her attitude becomes almost avoidant: When she catches herself stressing or overthinking, she quickly tries to flee the emotion. "Just stop. Just don't go there!" The trouble is, the price of this avoidance is a loss of awareness.

We can be aware without being anxious.

We can even be aware of anxiety without being anxious!

We can cultivate this awareness in ourselves by regularly "checking in" with our bodily sensations, thoughts, and feelings, by making sure that our lifestyle is supporting us in the ways we need it to, and by including some form of mindfulness in everyday life.

Picture this. It's the end of a long day and you're exhausted. You were late for the morning meeting and had an argument with a colleague. You were given too much work again. The builders outside have been making noise *all day long* and driving you crazy. Your to-do list is as long as you are and you feel close to the breaking point, when your boyfriend sends you a cryptic message saying you "need to talk."

When stress piles on in this way, it can feel utterly overwhelming. It's like playing an ultra-fast game of Tetris where you can't think straight because there's always another challenge, another crisis demanding your attention. Even though it can often feel like there's nothing you can do about stress (that thought alone is stressful!), there are always ways to stop, take a breath, and notice what's happening.

Anxiety: "There's so much going on right now, and I can't cope, and I'm about ready to scream! Nobody respects me. I can't do this anymore. What did his message mean? Why is this happening?"

Awareness: "There's a lot going on right now. My heart is racing and I'm beginning to panic. I can feel my thoughts racing."

Can you see the judgment, interpretation, and clinging anxiety? And can you see that in awareness, you don't lose any conscious perception of what is going on, but merely take it all in without attaching negative stories, judging, or resisting? Can you also see that in having awareness, you create a little opening and possibility for yourself to choose what you would like to do next, rather than just get carried away in a flurry of stress?

When we talk about stress-management, we are not necessarily talking about getting rid of stress entirely. It's impossible! And we're also not talking about numbing yourself out, becoming less perceptive, or being less aware. Rather, it's about being aware without attaching anxiety-provoking narratives and judgments to that awareness. If you can do this, then you can choose what you want to do about life's inevitable stresses. Let's look at what your options are.

The 4 A's of Stress Management

This technique was first proposed by the Mayo Clinic but has since been used in various iterations by therapists, coaches, doctors, and laypeople all over the world. Having a simple, structured approach to anxiety can be like a lifeboat in the storm of stress and overthinking. All you need to remember is four techniques: **avoid, alter, accept, and adapt.** It can be a comfort in itself to know that really, there are only these **four** possible ways to respond to any life stress.

The first thing you can do is **avoid.**

Sounds suspiciously simple, but there's a lot of aggravation in life you can simply walk away from. We can't control everything in life, but we can arrange our circumstances so that we don't have to be in stressful surroundings, or with stressful people. If we're honest, we might see that a lot of the stress in our lives is voluntary—and we don't have to agree to it!

Think about what is stressing you in your environment and how you can take control to moderate or remove it entirely. Consider someone who hates how busy the grocery stores are on Saturday morning. Knowing that this stresses them out, they can rearrange their schedule so they do their weekly shopping at the quietest time, say, on a Tuesday evening. There's no need to manage the stress of a busy supermarket if you just avoid it entirely.

You can avoid stressful people in exactly the same way. Do you find that your stress goes through the roof when your parents come to stay for the holidays? Find a way to have them stay in a nearby B&B, or avoid planning any activities where you are all alone together in a room for hours with nothing to do but stress each other out.

When you avoid stress, you are not running away from obligations or denying genuine problems. You are simply learning to say "no" to stress that is unnecessary and harmful. We can always say no to situations and people that demand too much of us and our resources. Those resources can be mental energy and attention, but they can also be time. If something in your life is gobbling up all your time, you *can* say no.

Look at your to-do list and get rid of the two or three items that are not urgent and not your priority. Delegate tasks or let someone else take on a responsibility. You don't have to do it all! So, the next time you face a stressful prospect, ask yourself, "Can I just avoid this whole thing?" If you can, do it.

If you can't, you might need to find ways to change the situation, i.e., **alter** it.

You always have the option of asking others to change their behavior. For example, if the builders are making a racket outside, politely ask them to pause for ten minutes while you finish an important phone call. Communicate your needs and feelings directly, rather than suffering in silence. If you never clearly tell your friend that his stupid jokes really hurt you, you may sit quietly and bear the brunt of it forever, when it would have been easy to tell him how you feel and ask him to stop.

We can't avoid every stress in life, but we often have a say in how these events unfold. Talk to people, negotiate, and use "I" statements to share your needs and ask for what you want. If you can't help but go to the store on Saturday morning, play your audiobook on your phone and listen to it while you shop, if it relaxes you. If you can't avoid that extra PTA meeting, try to lump it in with other errands you're already doing so you save time, effort, and potentially gas for your car. You can also do a lot to alter unavoidable situations by cutting them down to a more manageable size. If you can't get out of going to that boring party, go but be upfront in the beginning and say, "Unfortunately, I have to go in an hour—early start tomorrow!"

If you can't avoid a stressor, ask what you can do to change it.

If your answer is "not much," then you might need to go one step further and **accept** it.

How do you accept a situation you dislike? First, if you dislike it, then you dislike it. Acceptance doesn't mean pretending you don't feel how you feel; it's an acknowledgment that it's *okay* to feel that way. Validate your own emotions and own them. For example, your boyfriend has just broken up with you via text, and there's not much you can do about his decision. But you can work on accepting the situation by calling up a friend to share your feelings.

If the situation is one in which you've been wronged, acceptance may take the form of trying to find a way to forgive. Remember that forgiveness is something you do for yourself, not the other person. When you forgive, you are releasing yourself from the stress and energy of resenting and blaming the other person.

Acceptance may also be about the subtle shifts in the way we frame events. We can't change the events themselves, but we can watch how we talk about them inwardly and the language we use. For example, instead of saying, "I completely failed my course and wasted my money. I'm such an idiot for not working harder," you could say, "I made a mistake and I'm not happy about it. But this one event doesn't define me. I can learn from mistakes and move on. I can do better next time."

Acceptance doesn't mean we agree with what happened or that we like it and shouldn't try to change it. It only means we gracefully come to terms with what we can't realistically change, so we can focus on what we can.

In the longer term, we do our best in the face of stress if we can **adapt**. Adapting means making more lasting changes to our worldview, our goals, our perception and expectations. Picture someone who is a perfectionist and is always stressed out because they never seem to meet their high standards. The best approach isn't that they find a way to be Superman, but instead lower their expectations so they're more reasonable and in line with reality.

Adapting to stress means we change *ourselves* to better cope with life. You might simply refuse to engage in depressing thoughts and deliberately practice being more optimistic. When we alter our perspective, we can see things differently. Is this a "crisis" or a "challenge"? How does this obstacle look when we tell ourselves, "I'm a resilient person," compared to when we tell ourselves, "Life isn't fair; this will end badly like everything does"?

When we adapt to stress, we find ways to make ourselves stronger. We build a worldview for ourselves that empowers us. For example, someone might get into the habit of making a "gratitude list" every day of all the wonderful things they are actually blessed with in life. Another person might meditate on their own personal "code" or say a mantra daily to remind them that they are strong and they can get through adversity. If we have an arsenal of powerful attitudes, ideas, philosophies, and inspiration, we can go into the world knowing that we can handle stress—and maybe even be better people for it!

So, those are the four A's of stress management. When you find yourself feeling anxious, pause and run through each of them in sequence. No matter how stressful the situation, there is a way for you to engage with it mindfully and proactively. You are not helpless in the face of stress—you have tools at your disposal! To use these tools, all it takes is a little awareness.

For example, there may be a colleague at work who stresses you out daily. Instead of getting overwhelmed by telling yourself there's nothing you can do about it, pause and ask if you can simply *avoid* this colleague. Maybe you can have lunch at a different time to avoid meeting them in the cafeteria, or maybe you can physically move to work farther away from them. But let's say you can't avoid encountering them in weekly meetings, and this is where they frequently interrupt you or steal your ideas.

You think of ways to *alter* the situation. Can you get out of these meetings? Can you speak to your colleague privately and share your concerns ("I'm uncomfortable in meetings lately, and I feel dismissed when you interrupt me")? Can you speak up in meetings and assert a stronger boundary when you talk? If none of these are really possible, you can still *accept* the situation to some degree. You might confide in a close friend about your frustrations, or come to realize that this colleague actually interrupts everyone, so you won't continue to take it personally or let it stress you.

Finally, you can adapt by working on becoming an overall more confident and assertive person. When you genuinely feel that you have as much right to speak as anyone else, then you may feel more confident saying, "Sorry, I was still speaking," and carrying on calmly.

Stress Diaries and Journals

Another concrete way to bring more awareness to your daily experience of stress is to write it all down. With overthinking, it can sometimes seem like there are a million things on your plate at once, and it's hard to decide what single cause is really behind your anxiety.

In 2018, researchers Smythe et. al. at Pennsylvania State University found that positive affect journaling (or PAJ) was positively correlated with better emotional self-regulation, improved wellbeing, and fewer depression and anxiety symptoms one month after starting an online journaling program. To do this kind of journaling, simply write about a traumatic experience for no more than fifteen to twenty minutes for around three to five days. As you write, gradually shift your focus onto positive effects, i.e., good emotions. You can use prompts like:

What has someone done to help you?

What are you grateful for?

What are your ultimate values and principles?

So, you could use PAJ to unpack a horrible argument you've recently had with someone. You can sit down and first "vent" a little to put words to what you're feeling. For example, "I can't believe she'd say that, and I'm so hurt that she didn't consider how her words would affect me . . ." As you write, however, you could gradually start to reframe the stressful encounter in more positive terms. "I'm glad I was able to step away and cool off before I said something I regret. That's something to be proud of. And I suppose one good thing that has come from this is that we are finally having this difficult conversation we should have had years ago."

This way, you are putting your ruminative mind to work chewing over a stressful idea until you resolve it, rather than just chewing over it! Gently shifting your own perspective in a journal this way could lead to you being able to do it on the spur of the moment, as stressful events unfold. One interesting finding of the above study is that people who practiced this technique scored higher on a measure of emotional resiliency, i.e., they were more likely to believe that they were strong and able to recover from stressful events.

This is more evidence that avoiding anxiety by using common stress-busting techniques is not likely to work in the long run. Imagine that your overthinking and stressed-out mind is an excitable and disobedient greyhound. Then imagine that the above technique is a way to let the greyhound loose so that it can run dozens of laps around a big field, eventually tiring itself out.

Only once the greyhound is exhausted is it able to be trained. However, if your stress management technique is only able to keep the greyhound chained up somewhere, to keep the metaphor going, you may gain a little control in the short term, but the dog is as excitable as ever (maybe more so) and you never allow yourself to reach that point where, after you're mentally "exhausted," you can begin to think more clearly about the problem at hand.

The only trick with this approach, however, is to make sure that you are constantly moving toward something more positive. You are not just venting and complaining, but allowing your expression over time to be transformed into something healthier and more balanced. To do this, keep prompting yourself with the above questions. You might even ask yourself directly, "What good can come of all this? In what way is this situation a potential benefit to me?"

But this is not the only way to use journaling. **A stress diary can help you pinpoint your triggers, as well as your reaction to them**. From there, you can start taking active steps to manage your stress levels.

The reason Angie has been so unsuccessful in her de-stressing attempts is that, as we've seen, she is essentially avoiding her stressful thoughts rather than facing them head on. And because she avoids them, she loses awareness about what they actually are. This means that she knows she has a stress problem but has no idea where exactly the stress is coming from, why, how, or when. And that means she can't take even the first step to addressing the issue.

Angie might feel extremely frazzled, and when asked why, she simply says, "I don't know . . . work," or even something vaguer still, like, "Life!" But what is it exactly about work that is stressing her? She doesn't know.

A stress diary is simply a written record of your level of stress and the accompanying information, which you can analyze later and use to take steps to manage stress. A stress diary gives you objective, workable data. "I'm stressed" is not a detailed or nuanced enough insight to be of any *practical* use. This is the kind of observation that people can only shrug their shoulders at and respond, "Maybe try yoga?"

However, "I find it very difficult to have several Zoom meetings in a row, and find that they really overwhelm and agitate me at work," is different—the detail and specificity of this problem allows us to see a potential solution going forward.

In fact, you can probably see that the thought, "I'm stressed," is only likely to create more stress precisely because nothing concrete can be done about the observation, whereas, "I have trouble with Zoom meetings," is a more definite awareness that is likely to curtail anxiety rather than create more of it.

The idea is simple: for each entry in your stress diary, record the time and date and how you're feeling at that moment. A common way to do this is on a rating scale (for example, one for not stressed at all and ten for super stressed), but you can also use feeling words, or note physical symptoms (like sweaty palms). Also note how effective and productive you're feeling using a scale as well. Then, note any stressful events that have recently happened as well as any ideas for what you feel could be the causes of your current state. Try to build a three-dimensional snapshot of what your anxiety and overthinking actually look like. Finally, note how you responded to the event and what the overall outcome was.

The stress diary alone represents a key mindset shift in how you approach anxiety. Instead of noticing stress and overthinking and then running away from it screaming (like Angie), you get curious. Instead of saying, "Something bad is happening; it has to stop," and doing whatever you can to evade that sensation, you are simply interested in asking what *is* happening?

For example:

4 February, 9:15

Received a worrying message about Dad needing surgery on his shoulder. Feeling around 4/10, kind of apprehensive and a little tired. Weird knot feeling in my stomach. Trouble staying focused on work: only working at about 1/10 effectiveness. I think I feel this way because I'm worried about something bad happening to him. I'm avoiding replying to the message, but I think this is making my anxiety worse.

Make an entry every time you feel your mood shifting, or when you're noticeably stressed. Track any big, emotional shifts or noteworthy events. Try to keep judgment and interpretation out of it—you are only gathering data. Become aware, as you write in your diary, that *noticing* anxiety is not necessarily the same as *engaging* with it.

Keep a stress diary for a few days or a week, and then sit down to analyze it and find any patterns:

1. What are the most frequent causes of stress, i.e., what usually comes before a sudden rise in stress or drop in mood?
2. How do these events typically affect your productivity?
3. How do you normally respond to these events, emotionally and behaviorally, and is your approach working?

4. Can you identify a level of stress that was comfortable and beneficial for your productivity?

This last point brings to attention something we can easily forget in our blind hurry to de-stress: We all need *some* stress in life! A stress diary can help you identify your optimal range. So for example, you might notice that you are at a stress level of around 2 or 3 out of 10, but that this level is relatively comfortable and a zone where you are at your most productive and efficient. You can learn not only the *level* of stress that works best for you, but also the *kind* of stress that is beneficial. This is a vital insight you would not get without taking the time to keep a stress diary.

When you analyze your stress diary like this, you are working with real data that can help you make insightful changes. You may even be surprised at some findings—only in writing things down in the moment do you see clear patterns emerge.

As you're analyzing, avoid overanalyzing! Remember that the goal of the stress journal is not to catch yourself out or feel bad about what you discover. In other words, there should be no judgment. Instead take a compassionate, curious approach and stay open-minded. Overthinkers are typically intelligent, but sometimes that just means they're really good at hiding obvious things from themselves!

You don't need to keep a stress diary forever. In fact, after using it a few weeks, the process might become automatic and you may develop more spontaneous awareness in the moment, as stress is occurring. You might be in traffic one day and notice that every time you're in a jam, it seems to set off the same chain reaction of thoughts. If this happens often enough, you may gain awareness even before you end up in the next traffic jam, and suddenly that window of awareness opens up, and you now have the choice: do you *want* to go down that same path of overthinking? Especially since you know where it goes?

Once you have a handle on the real causes of stress in your life, you can use something like the 4 A's technique to take action, or else rearrange your lifestyle or schedule to moderate stress. If you notice that all of your stress is coming from one person, you can draw some boundaries around your relationship. If you notice that your normal response of getting angry tends to make things harder to handle, you can begin to work on your anger. If your job is a continued source of worry, you can gauge how bad it is and take action both short term (taking a holiday) or longer term (considering getting a different job).

The format described above isn't the only way that writing things down can help. You can keep a more traditional journal and explore your feelings more generally, whether occasionally or every day. Writing things down can relieve stress on its own, but it can also help you gather your thoughts, hash out problems, find insights, and process any issues you're going through. It's like your journal is an informal therapist!

Use journaling or diaries according to what you like and what works in your situation. If you're battling low mood and find your anxiety is general and seems to affect everything, you might find a gratitude journal helpful. Simply list five things daily that you are thankful for, even if it's nothing more exciting than your morning cup of coffee or the fact that you have a nice new pair of socks. This can subtly shift your focus onto your resources and possibilities and reframe your experience.

If you are processing some traumatic life event or are going through a very difficult time, you might like to journal simply as an emotional release. "Dump" all your feelings onto paper and work through them. Once down on paper, you might start naturally gaining some self-knowledge, or see some hints for ways forward.

If the stress in your life is more ongoing, you might like to try bullet journaling, where you use brief notes to keep track of daily goals, priorities, and memories. Keeping things brief can help you stay organized and add structure to your life. Some people like to bring an artistic element to bullet journaling and use color and pictures to express themselves and gather inspiration, encouraging positive feelings. Others use pre-made journals with prompts printed inside them.

Journals and diaries are not for everyone, though. Skip them if they only seem to make your perfectionism worse, or if you find yourself agonizing over the right technique. The journal is just a tool to get closer to your emotions—if you find yourself focusing more on the journal than your emotions, you might need to try a different technique. Try to finish every journaling session with something positive and grounding—recite a mantra, visualize something positive, or consider some possibilities and solutions going forward. If you don't make sure to return to a positive headspace, journaling may start to feel like it only encourages more unhappiness and overthinking.

The 5-4-3-2-1 Grounding Technique

Stress journals and the 4 A's technique can be used to great effect when paired together, especially if done regularly. But sometimes, you need a technique that will bring *immediate* relief to a stressful situation. While the previous two techniques are a great way of cultivating and using awareness, they are not so useful if your problem is gaining awareness in the first place. If you've ever been trapped in an "anxiety spiral," you'll know that pulling yourself out of it can be nearly impossible.

The following technique is often used by those who experience panic attacks; it's a way to halt the anxiety spiral before it runs away with you. You don't have to have a panic disorder to benefit, though. Overthinking runs on all the same machinery as more complex fears and phobias do, and it can be reined in in the same way.

The idea is simple: when we overthink and ruminate and stress, we are *out of the moment*. We chew on thoughts of the past or entertain possibilities in the future. We think about "what if" and run our minds ragged on memories, ideas, probabilities, wishes, and fears. If we can pull our conscious awareness *back into the present*, we can halt some of this overthinking. And we can do this by checking in with the five senses. To put it another way, the brain can carry you all over the place, but the body—and its senses—is only ever one place: the present.

In moments of panic, we can get really caught up in ideas and thoughts, even though in reality, we are perfectly safe and sound and there is nothing in our immediate situation to threaten us. With panic, however, we can be sitting in perfect peace in a sunny garden somewhere and nevertheless feel like we're going to die. Such is the power of the mind!

The next time you feel anxiety and panic spiraling out of control, try this: stop, take a breath, and look around you.

- First, find five things in your environment that you can see. You might rest your eyes on the lamp in the corner, your own hands, a painting on the wall. Take a moment to really look at all these things: their textures, colors, shapes. Take your time to run your eyes over every inch and take it all in.

- Next, try to find four things in your environment that you can feel or touch. Feel the weight of your body against the chair, or the texture of the jacket you're wearing, or reach out to feel how cool and smooth the glass of the car window feels against your fingers.
- Next, find three things that you can hear. Your own breath. The distant sound of traffic or birds.
- Next, find two things you can smell. This might be tricky at first, but notice that everything has a smell if you pay attention. Can you smell the soap on your skin or the faint earthy smell of the paper on your desk?
- Finally, find one thing that you can taste. Maybe the lingering flavor of coffee on your tongue. Even if you can't find anything, just dwell for a moment on what your taste buds are sensing. Are they really "off" or does your mouth almost have a taste of its own when you stop to become aware of it? Stay there for a moment and explore that sensation.

The point of this exercise is, on the surface, distraction. While your senses are active, your brain is engaged in something other than endless rumination, and your overthinking is halted. You put a spanner in the works and stop runaway thoughts. Practice this technique often enough and you may notice that it instantly calms you and slows you down.

In the moment, you might not remember which sense comes next, but this isn't important. What matters is that you are giving your full and focused attention to something outside of yourself and letting anxious energy dissipate. It's difficult to stop a thought by saying, "I think I should stop thinking," because, obviously, this itself is a thought. But if you can put your brain on pause and re-engage your senses for a moment, you unhook yourself from the worry track and give yourself a moment to become present and calm.

Think of it this way: your conscious being can only do one thing at a time, either having thoughts or being immersed in the moment via the senses. It's one or the other. If you can tether your consciousness to the present moment using your senses, it is difficult for your mind to simultaneously run all over the place in anxious overthinking.

If all of the above sounds too complicated to remember in the moment, try this: literal grounding. Researcher Gaétan Chevalier found that "earthing" or grounding the human body on the actual earth had fascinating effects on mood. Chevalier asked participants of the study to put their feet or bodies in contact with the earth for one hour. He then tested them and found a statistically significant boost in the self-reported moods and levels of wellbeing in those who were in contact with the earth versus those who spent the hour without this contact. Though grounding in this way is unlikely to be enough to combat a more serious anxiety disorder, it's certainly an encouraging finding. If you can, try the 5-4-3-2-1 technique outdoors, where your bare feet are in contact with the soil.

Narrative Therapy and Externalization

A final technique we'll consider comes from the world of narrative therapy, which explores the way that our lives are often construed as stories, or narratives. People are meaning-making machines, and we make meaning by telling stories about who we are and what the events of our lives signify. With narrative therapy, we can essentially rewrite these stories to find healing and, well, a happy ever after!

We've already discussed that a big part of overcoming anxiety is to look at our mental models and consciously make decisions about how we want to run our lives. When we are the narrator of our own stories, we take charge, reframe, and are empowered to make new meanings. The big tenet behind narrative therapy is that people are separate from their problems, and indeed this idea underpins a popular technique called "externalization."

When we externalize, we put the problem *out there*. We are not wrong or bad to have problems, and we don't judge or blame ourselves for having them. Nevertheless, we do have the power to change how we talk about ourselves and our lives, and we can make meaningful changes. So, when it comes to overthinking, a big step is saying, "Overthinking is a problem, and I'm going to find alternatives," versus saying, "I am an overthinker and that's bad. I have to find a way to fix myself." Another big step is to realize that you really are in control and are the *author* of your own experience—other people are not to blame for our perception, and equally they cannot save or teach us; we are the experts of our own experience.

Our mental models are a little like patterns or filters or repeating motifs. If your life was a movie, what genre would it be? What role would you always play, and how would the story play out? When we can see that our interpretations and frames influence our experience, we are empowered to change them for ourselves. For example, overthinkers tend to feel powerless, but what if they changed the story and saw themselves as being responsible and capable?

Let's return to externalization. You are not your problems. You are not your failures. If you can put distance between yourself and your life challenges, you gain perspective and untangle your sense of identity and self-worth from the temporary moment you're experiencing. Just like a cloud is not the sky, our problems are not who we are—they will pass, and we do have control over how we respond to them.

If you're feeling overwhelmed, it may help to repeat the mantra to yourself: "I am not my problems." Change your language, too. Instead of, "I'm an anxious person," say, "I'm experiencing anxiety right now," or even, "I'm noticing some anxiety." We can put distance between ourselves and our problems in many ways:

- Use the journaling or stress diary techniques above. Take the anxiety out of your head and put it down on a piece of paper. Burn the paper, or scrunch it up and throw it away. Physically see that the problem is separate from you, and from a distance, you can take action to change it.

- Use visualization and imagery. Visualize all the overthinking as air inside you that you blow into a giant balloon, and then imagine the balloon floating up and away from you, getting smaller and smaller. Really enjoy the sensation that you don't have to fully *identify* with your worries; you can put them down sometimes, and you can walk away to get perspective. Imagine the balloon disappearing out of sight, along with your worries. Another technique is to imagine yourself putting your worries away in a locked safe before going to bed. Tell yourself, "I can always open the safe and come and get these later if I want to, but for now, I'm sleeping."

- If you're inclined to, use creativity to externalize: write, draw, paint, or even sing and dance your problems, and make them real outside of your body. Some people give their judgmental or overly paranoid inner voice a name so they can say, "Oh yes, this isn't *me*. That's just boring old Fred again, overthinking as usual. Hi, Fred!"

Another technique used in narrative therapy is deconstruction. When you overthink, the sensation is often one of overwhelm: there are a million things going on in your head, all at a thousand miles an hour, and you don't even know where to start with any of it. The great thing about a story, however, is that it's sequential. It's one step after another. If we're feeling lost in rumination, we can use stories to help us break down (or deconstruct) a big, scary problem into smaller, easier ones.

A story is a way to organize, to slow things down, and to remind you that you are in control when it comes to where and how you place your attention. You cannot look at *everything* all at once. Trying to do so often makes you feel powerless and small in the face of overwhelming thoughts. But, as in any good story, you don't have to figure everything out immediately or solve every problem all at one time. Some ways to bring deconstruction into your own life:

- If things are feeling disastrous, stop and force yourself to focus on the *single thing* that is most important right now. If you're catastrophizing about things that may happen tomorrow or next year or whenever, set those aside and look at what matters today only, or perhaps only what matters in this very moment. Ask yourself, what single next step can you take? Don't worry about the next twenty steps, just take the next step you need to, and then you can go from there.

- If you find yourself returning to distressing memories from the past, take a moment to deliberately lay out your history, perhaps even writing it down or laying it out on a chart. Break down events into episodes and look for themes, patterns, and a thread that links them all together. See how the present moment ties into the past, then ask yourself what you can do to take charge of your own narrative. For example, if you're cringing over mistakes you made in the past, you might construct a story where you weren't just an idiot who did something wrong, but you were young and learning, and in your development, you're continually getting better. You can see that your embarrassment now is proof of you being a more mature person. You can see the *whole picture*—one of growth and progress. Doesn't that feel better than simply churning over a humiliating comment you made once in fifth grade?

- Anxiety and overthinking have a way of "fracturing" our attention and creating chaos and confusion. When we deconstruct all of these thoughts, however, we see that many of them are just noise, and we don't necessarily have to entertain them. Maybe you're primarily concerned about your health, and off that single worry branches a million other thoughts of losing your job, dying, expensive medical bills, etc. Deconstructing these means asking, "What is this thought really about?" and distinguishing thoughts that derail and distract from those where you can actually make meaningful changes.

Takeaways

- Now that we've identified what overthinking is, we need to know how to combat it. There are many things you can do to de-stress and calm an anxious, overthinking mind that are simple yet effective.
- The first thing you need to remember is a mantra called the 4 A's of stress management. These are avoid, alter, accept, and adapt. Avoiding things entails simply walking away from things you can't control. Some things are simply not worth the effort and are best removed from our environments altogether. However, if we can't avoid it, we must learn how to alter our environment to remove the stressor. If we can't alter our environment, we have no choice but to accept it. Lastly, if we can't do much about the situation at all, we must adapt to it and learn how to cope with our stressor and reduce its damaging potential to a minimum.

- Another popular technique is journaling. When we overthink, we have tons of different thoughts swirling in our mind, which can feel overwhelming. However, when we write these down systematically, we can analyze them and evaluate whether these thoughts are merited at all. To build the habit, you can carry a pocket journal with you and write whenever you feel it's necessary.
- A third technique we have is called the 5-4-3-2-1 technique. This is highly effective at stemming panic attacks, and it does so by involving all five of our senses. So, whenever you feel panic overcoming you, look for five things around you that you can see, four things you can touch, three that you can smell, two that you can hear, and one that you can taste. Engaging your senses distracts your brain from overthinking.

Chapter 3. Manage Your Time and Inputs

Susie has a lot to do today. She looks at her schedule and wonders with some panic how she is going to fit everything in. Her work colleague, seeing her overstressed and sinking into anxious overthinking, steps in with a suggestion—why not do a little lunchbreak meditation? Meditation has been proven to lower stress levels, right? But five minutes into meditation, Susie is screaming inside and realizing that she now has even less time than before and can't focus because all she can think about is that appointment she has at 2:30.

The classic relaxation techniques many people suggest are no help if the **cause of our stress is actually poor time management**. Susie would benefit from only two things—a magical way to add more hours to the day, or a schedule that better manages her time! While meditation, stretching, and so on can help us deal with the inevitable stress that's on our plates, we can also minimize the stress we're exposed to in the first place by better managing our time. This chapter is all about smart and proven techniques for taking control in this way.

Stress Management 101

For many of us, good stress management is simply good time management. If you find yourself anxious about deadlines, feel rushed, too busy or overwhelmed, then you may derive more from time management strategies than techniques aimed directly at relaxation.

A study published in the *European Journal of Psychology of Education* tentatively found that university students' stress levels could be lowered when their time management skills were improved, even as their study demands stayed the same. The key, they found, was that *perceived* stress was reduced, even if the facts of their schedules remained unchanged. In a 2021 PLOS meta-analysis, Brad Aeon and colleagues actually found in their research that while time management improves work performance and achievement, its greatest effect is improving overall wellbeing and life satisfaction.

Time management, in turn, often comes down to one fundamental skill: identifying your priorities and using them to guide your goal-setting. When you can do this, you increase feelings of competence and control and indirectly boost your resilience when inevitable setbacks occur. As usual, it all comes down to both awareness and mindset.

It's weird, when you think about it, just how many of us *prioritize stress* in our lives. We allocate all our available time to activities that worsen our mood and leave us feeling anxious or depleted, while putting recuperation and contemplation way at the bottom of the list, if we think about it at all. When was the last time you deliberately prioritized rest and relaxation? If you're like most people, you always put hard work first and give the crumbs of your time and energy to everything else. Then, you might be like Susie who desperately tries to squeeze in a healthy meditation class but only ends up resenting it because it's yet one more thing on the to-do list.

One mindset shift is to see rest and relaxation as important and worthy of your focus, and not just something you tack onto the end of a day once more important things are done. One way to do this is to schedule in time for fun and enjoyable activities, or simply time when you're not doing anything at all. A positive attitude is one of your most valuable resources in life—why not take care of it and nurture these good feelings proactively?

Overthinkers can sometimes have problems with being over responsible. They may unconsciously downplay their own wellbeing or pleasure and believe that all the serious and unpleasant work of life has to be the first focus, and relaxing is a rare treat they can only earn when everything else in life is checked off the list (i.e., never!).

Stress management is about removing those unnecessary stressors, but it's also about proactively making room for those things in life that we enjoy and which refresh and regenerate us. You could begin the day with something enjoyable, rather than dive into chores and stressful tasks. Make a habit of taking ten-minute breaks every hour for a nice cup of herbal tea, a stretch, or a little walk. Have something to look forward to every day, and foster connections with people you care about and who make your life a brighter place. Take time to laugh a little, to play and joke, and to do something simply because it makes you happy.

You already know about the lifestyle changes you need to make to support yourself physically and cut stress: sleep well, lower caffeine intake, exercise, eat properly, and so on. But your social, emotional, and spiritual health are important too. If you don't deliberately take time to engage in these things, they simply won't get done.

Remember Susie? She sits down every morning and writes out her to-do list, working in all her important tasks from her schedule. But when it comes to working out, spending time with friends or family, or doing things she loves, she puts these far, far down the list, and so they never get done. Instead, she could proactively decide that relationships, physical health, and enjoyment are important in life, and that she will dedicate some time every day to them. If there's not enough time in the day for all that *and* her work? That means her work isn't right for her.

Time management is not just a superficial way to juggle the chores of the day. It's a way to structure your entire life and manage the architecture of your living so that you spend your resources and energy on those things that matter most. It's not just about squeezing as much work into the day as you possibly can, but about balance and looking at your life with the knowledge that its proportions and priorities reflect your values.

Let's be honest: there is always going to be something new to demand your attention and hog your time. It's up to us to consciously steer the direction of life so that we make the most of the time and energy we have. Here's a great general framework for how to do this:

1. Decide on your values and priorities in life. What three things matter most to you?

2. Observe for a week the way you spend the time available to you. Log every hour and what you do with it.

3. Analyze this data: where do you spend the most time? And least time? Finally, look to see if how you actually spend time reflects your values. For example, if you most care about your family, building your own business, and staying fit, does it make sense that you spend

ninety percent of your waking hours on work alone?

4. Guided by your values and principles, restructure your schedule to better reflect your priorities.

5. Observe again to see how you're doing, what's working, and what adjustments you can make.

As an example, you may discover that you highly value contemplative alone time, your independence, and the opportunity to be creative and make art. You observe yourself for a week and notice that you spend a tiny fraction of your waking hours on these three values, and most of your time on distracting media and dealing with demanding clients after hours.

For you, stress management will not be a question of learning to find room in your life for hours of daily social media and TV use, or innovative ways to accommodate pushy clients. Rather, stress management will look like gently restricting your life so you have more of what makes you happy and less of what doesn't. Perhaps you implement a "no phones or TV after 5 p.m." rule at home, or set up a "not in the office" automated email for clients who push boundaries.

There's no point talking about time management without knowing what your goals and priorities are. Good time management depends entirely on the outcomes you're aiming for, and you need to know what you value first. With your values in mind, you can start to decide what's important and what isn't; i.e., you can rank activities and tasks.

Begin every day with your priorities, which get most of your attention, time, and resources. In the morning, write a to-do list for the day. Take a look at the items and rank them: **urgent**, **important**, or **not important**. Urgent items need to be done today and take priority. Defer these and you invite stress. Important tasks are a little less urgent and often include "life maintenance" tasks that, when not done, cause problems, like taking out the trash.

Not important tasks can wait, or are not priorities. You can decide on your own ranking system and make your own definition for what "important" really means to you, but clarify it for yourself before assigning each label to a task. Some people find it useful to limit the number of urgent or important tasks, i.e., they ask, "What three things are going to be my focus for today?" and then they relax on the other, less important tasks.

There are several tips, tricks, and techniques for the detailed management of your time, and many clever apps and methods designed to help streamline the process. But if you follow the above fundamentals, you can make your time work for you. A good time management habit will reflect your unique lifestyle and goals, but there are a few things to keep in mind:

- Writing things down makes them more concrete—have a to-do list, calendar, schedule, or something physical to note your goals daily and track progress.

- Break bigger tasks into smaller ones and set mini-goals on the way to your bigger ones.

- Think process rather than outcome. If you focus on daily helpful habits, you'll achieve more in the long term than if you focused on quick results and perfectionism.

- Get used to saying no to things that are not important. It's okay to delegate or draw a boundary to respect your limits.

- Continually weight up your actions to your bigger goals and ask, does this bring me closer or take me further away? Then act accordingly.

Of course, laying it out like this makes time management seem simple—and it *is* simple, but not always easy. Despite knowing better, we sometimes hold on to old patterns of behavior that work against us. If we know what these roadblocks are, however, we can pre-empt them and work around them. Why do some time management techniques work for some people and not others? Well, because we're not all the same, and we don't all face the same challenges.

There are not just time management techniques, but individual time management styles or personas. How you manage your own time (or fail to, for that matter) may come down to some unique differences in your own history and personality.

For example, the **time martyr** is the person who accepts everyone else's request and takes on too much obligation and responsibility—then suffers for it. For example, you agree to meet three different friends one after the other on the same day despite knowing it will be a mad dash to get it done. At the end of the day, you're frazzled and find yourself triggered into overthinking ("Was I a little rude with my friend when we said goodbye? Maybe I was too curt and she noticed and maybe she's mad at me now.").

If this is you, you might gain a surface sense of pride at being so busy, but you're not tackling what's genuinely important to you. Good techniques for you would be anything that cuts down on distractions and multitasking—such as a strict schedule or a limit to complete only three main tasks per day.

The **procrastinator** has different challenges: delaying any action at all until it's often too late. While some pressure is good, for the procrastinator, anxiety only impairs them further. You might not think that procrastination and overthinking have much to do with each other, but consider the person who has put off work they know they should do, and the stress this creates.

If you procrastinate, you may benefit from breaking things down into small tasks and rewarding yourself for each mini-milestone.

The **distractor** has a related problem—they start but are often derailed by distractions and find their attention going all over the place. Distraction and overthinking can feed each other into epic proportions. What works for people with this tendency is to have firmer boundaries and a better consideration for the kind of environment they work in. For example, you might decide to drastically declutter your office and set a firm boundary not to be disturbed during certain work hours. This will reduce the number of things that pop up and demand your attention, triggering stress and overthinking.

The **underestimator** mistakenly thinks tasks will take less time than they really do, and they can miss deadlines because their estimations were too optimistic. Here, time management also comes down to building in ample time for tackling projects step by step, to give time to appraise the process more realistically. This is a relatively easy issue to fix, but unresolved, it can wreak havoc.

The **firefighter** is always in a reactive state of mind, putting out "fires" all over and juggling a thousand things at once, often when a situation has reached a crisis point. To prevent burnout, such a person could learn to delegate more effectively and better distinguish between issues that are important and those that are urgent.

Constantly rushing to solve problems could be a sign that you're not doing what you should in the early stages and letting things get out of hand until they're much harder to keep control of. Think about someone who is so distracted and overwhelmed with panicking about Problem A that they completely overlook an important task about Problem B, creating trouble for themselves down the line. When they turn to Problem B without adequately resolving Problem A, the same thing happens.

The **perfectionist**, like the procrastinator, doesn't get things done because nothing ever matches up to their image of the perfect outcome. Often, though, the truth is that perfectionism is hiding a fear of finishing, or an intolerance of "good enough" outcomes that fall along a learning curve. This is the person who spends so long brainstorming the perfect birthday gift that by the time they decide, it's too late. Boundary setting, realistic planning, and delegating can help.

Whether you identify with one or more of the above, or find that your time management style is something else completely, it's useful to understand how you are currently acting so you can take steps to improve. Notice patterns and ask, what is hindering me from managing my time better right now? After all, any time management technique is only useful if it actually works for *you*, in *your* life.

How to Manage Your Time, Energy, and Inputs

Let's take a closer look at some of the strategies that might help you overcome your unique time management limitations. Bearing in mind your own time management personality and your lifestyle, you could try the following on for size.

Allen's Input Processing Technique
This technique is great for procrastinators, firefighters, and distractors, but can be helpful for anyone who wants to navigate our information-saturated world. In this technique, data is broadly called "inputs," i.e., any stimulus from the environment: meetings, emails, phone calls, social media, TV, other people, and so on. How do you respond to each of these little hooks that reaches out to grab your attention? Allen's technique claims that unless you plan ahead for how you respond, you're probably doing it sub-optimally.

With a plan, you don't have to waste precious time and energy scanning each new input as it comes along; you just make a quick decision and move on to what's really important. First, start by observing your day-to-day life and see if you identify your primary inputs. It doesn't really matter what they are, but that they grab your attention. Next, the big question: how do you respond? *Will you act because of this input?*

You need to decide if an input warrants your action, yes or no. If no, you can do it later or simply ignore it completely. If yes, then you act. Sounds easy, right? The trouble is letting inputs accumulate and cause you stress. For example, a letter comes in the mail, you open it, then set it aside. You pick it up later, read it again, but set it aside again on the other side of your desk. You might give your attention to this single letter four or five times before you finally act—and all that time you were slightly stressed out by it! Far better to pick it up and make an immediate decision—let's say you decide the letter must go into the trash, and that's that. Your workspace is clearer, and so is your mind.

If you must act, ask if you have to do it *right away*. Complete urgent tasks immediately, but if something has to be done later, don't just set it aside so it can sit nagging at the back of your mind. You could immediately schedule in a time on your to-do list for when you will tackle it, or set a reminder. Be specific about what needs to be done and when, or even delegate it entirely. Then, forget about it. A note-keeping phone app or calendar can help with this, but what's most important is that you are consistent.

The idea is that if you streamline your process this way, you are actually freeing up your attention and energy—and this results in you feeling calmer and more in control (which you are!). You'll overthink less because there will be less to think about, and you'll overall feel that things are less overwhelming and chaotic.

You need to be consistent. Stay on top of things and simply refuse to allow tasks to pile up. Pounce on any new issue that puts demands on your attention and make a decision on how you will act as early as possible: Is following this link your friend messaged you a priority right now? Is that email you received from your bank important? What is the quickest way to deal with the fact that you've just run out of milk?

Busy people can sometimes act against themselves: they're so flustered that they actually put off important tasks, which then become critical tasks, which then cause them far more stress than if they had dealt with them swiftly the moment they first appeared.

Eisenhower's Method
As the above method might have convinced you, good time management sooner or later comes down to knowing your own priorities and letting that guide your actions and goal-setting. The following method is great for firefighters, perfectionists, and time martyrs, since it forces us to efficiently tackle a task when we might not actually have the time or resources to do it properly.

A lot of overthinking comes down to juggling too many commitments with too little time or resources. This causes stress, which fuels overthinking. If we cannot avoid such time stress, we can certainly change it or adapt ourselves. Sadly, many of us do have too much to do in too little time. Former US President Eisenhower's Urgent/Important technique can help and let you cut through what truly matters and what is just acting as a distraction.

Important tasks are those that have outcomes that bring us closer to our goal.

Urgent tasks are those that need immediate attention, often since there is a penalty for not doing so.

This distinction is what's usually missing in a firefighter's mindset, since they will see *every* task as urgent when it isn't. You can start the technique by listing out the tasks and activities ahead of you, either for the day or the week. Now, assign each task one of four possible labels:

- important and urgent
- important but not urgent
- not important but urgent
- and not important and not urgent.

Next, rank these tasks—in the above given order.

For important and urgent tasks: *Do immediately*. These are your priority. It's a good idea to have some time every day scheduled for unforeseen events, but re-evaluate if there are many of these, and try to see how you could have planned for them.

For important but not urgent tasks: *Make a decision about when to do it*. These are the tasks that are essential for your long-term goals, but there isn't necessarily a big emergency requiring you to do them right now. Things like daily exercise, sorting your budget, maintaining relationships, etc. ought to be done diligently, but you can be a little flexible about *when*. The last thing you want is for them to become urgent—so act before they do. Try to schedule routine activities so you don't need to really think about them; for example, a morning run, a budget session every Sunday evening, or a weekly call with your mom.

For not important but urgent tasks: *Try to delegate*. These are the things that are pressing you but don't actually enrich your life or bring you closer to your goals. It's better if you can reschedule or delegate so you can spend time on things that actually do relate to your goals. Have good boundaries and say no to unnecessary commitments.

For not important and not urgent tasks: *Delete*! There's no need to waste time or effort on these things; just ignore or move on from them as quickly as possible and try to reduce their frequency in the future if you can. Things like pointless internet distractions, junk TV, gaming, and mindless social media can fall into this category.

Let's see how we might apply this approach to everyday life. Mike runs a small business—but it's rapidly growing. He is busy seemingly all the time. To keep a lid on his stress levels, he commits to becoming more aware of his current time managements habits, the tasks coming his way, and how the Eisenhower method might streamline it all.

In the morning, he sits down and writes a to-do list of the day's tasks. He puts down everything that's weighing on his mind, from the big and scary to the minute and mundane details at the edge of his awareness. Then he goes through the list and labels every item on it from 1 to 4, like so:

1. important and urgent—do immediately
2. important but not urgent—schedule action
3. not important but urgent—delegate
4. not important and not urgent—delete or ignore

One task is to respond to an email from a local charity that is asking him if he'd be interested in sponsoring a local event. This email arrived early in the morning and was even titled "please respond urgently" in the heading. Mike thinks for a moment: Is responding to this email *important*? In other words, does it help bring him closer to his goals? Seeing as his main business goal is to start scaling up his business within the next six months, then the answer is a clear no.

Now, this is not to say that the charity itself isn't important to Mike personally, or that it has no value or won't be important to someone else. It's not about the validity of the request, either. Rather, it's about priorities and deliberate focus. Mike then asks if the task is *urgent*. Is there a penalty for not answering this email quickly? The answer is also no.

He immediately knows what to do about this task—delegate it to his PA, giving him instructions to politely decline or defer.

Next, he considers the task of getting in touch with a new potential investor and arranging a meeting—this particular person is in fact only in town for the next week or so, making it an urgent task. The task is clearly important, too, as it will have a direct impact on the ultimate goal. He writes "1" beside it and decides that this will in fact be his first task of the day.

The next item is a little trickier—attending a ninety-minute gym session. Is this *important*? Well, it doesn't directly bring Mike closer to his goal of growing his business. But then again, he also knows that the healthier and fitter he is, the more energy he has for his business and the better his overall mood. So, it is important.

But is it *urgent*? Not really. He has to go at some point, but there's no urgency about it. He writes

"2" next to this item and schedules it after he has finished all his number "1" tasks. Mike works through the entire list and finds with relief that one quarter of it is slashed away (that's the number 4 tasks, which are neither important nor urgent) and all the number 3 tasks have been delegated or trimmed down to size.

He creates a new to-do list that is not only shorter but ranked. Mike reminds himself what his ultimate purpose is and realigns with that purpose by taking actions that will bring him closer to that goal. This instantly makes him feel calmer because he is more in control. He can quickly do away with pointless distractions while at the same time throwing all of his energy into the things that really matter. For Mike, **the way to have less stress in life is not to work less or to work harder, but to work more strategically.**

If Mike *hadn't* tried this technique, he may have gotten distracted by the early morning email from the charity, then got stuck writing and re-writing a complicated email response. He then might have paused this task while it was still unfinished (creating something undone that "hangs over him" and creates mild stress) when he remembers he needed to call the investor to arrange a meeting.

In a panic, he calls the investor and bumbles through the conversation, causing more stress. He returns to the email and tries to finish it off, along with a hundred other things he's been procrastinating all week. He quickly realizes that he'd better get to the gym before he runs out of time, but spends the whole session worrying about the awkward call with the investor— resulting in yet more stress and a very distracted and inefficient workout. At the end of the day, Mike feels rushed and chaotic but has actually accomplished *less* than he would have by being more focused, and at the same time, he brought extra unnecessary stress into his life.

Using this technique doesn't absolve you from acting quickly sometimes, taking responsibility, or putting off one task in favor of another. But it does put you in control to prioritize and organize these tasks, meaning you are less flustered and therefore experience less anxiety. Remember, the more in control you feel, the less likely you are to overthink or overanalyze. Instead, you use the analytical power of your brain to conduct a kind of "mental triage." Before anything is allowed to take up room in your head or in your schedule, examine it and ask whether it's a) important and b) urgent. Only *then* do you decide how much of your cognitive bandwidth and time to devote to it.

It can help to look at a task and literally say to it, "I'm going to put you out of my mind now because you are not necessary to my long-term goals and you are not urgent. I'm putting my attention elsewhere." Simply being decisive like this has a magical way of calming your nerves.

You can use this technique to assess your overall organization, or on a shorter timescale with your daily to-do list. As you work through tasks, ask yourself:

- Do I really need to be optimizing here, or is the best thing to do simply to eliminate it completely?
- Does this activity build toward my goals, satisfy my values, or fit with my ideal vision of myself?
- Even if I need to tackle this task now, do I need to tackle *all* of it now? What part of this task is truly important?

Sometimes, certain tasks have a way of convincing us that they're important and urgent when they really aren't. A demanding and boundary-violating friend may use guilt and obligation to convince you that his emergency is also your emergency; advertisers are well-known for creating a false sense of urgency, and even some productivity apps and tools falsely position themselves as important when they are actually the same old distractions in a new package. The good news is that the more often you remind yourself of *your* goals, *your* genuine values, and *your* priorities, the easier it gets and the quicker you can see through unreasonable demands on your attention.

Setting SMART Goals

You're probably already somewhat familiar with the concept of good goals being those that are specific and time limited, or so-called SMART goals. In Jan O'Neill's seminal work, *The Power of SMART Goals: Using Goals to Improve Student Learning*, she explores the evidence behind the relationship between clear, achievable goals and measurable success. O'Neill and several other education experts find again and again that the focus required to set concrete goals is the single biggest predictor for their fulfilment. Motivational speaker Tony Robbins is often credited with saying that goal-setting is "the first step in turning the invisible into the visible"—in other words, they carry us from the potential to the actual.

But when it comes to overthinking, we can look at goal-setting not just for its power to help us succeed. Goal-setting matters because a huge source of anxiety and rumination is uncertainty, lack of clarity, and diffused possibility. On the other hand, the more proactively we engage with the unknown (i.e., by making goals to shape it), the more in control we'll feel. If somebody is unclear on their path and their values, they are likely to feel overwhelmed and anxious even with low levels of stress, whereas someone who knows exactly what they want and why can seemingly dig deep and plough through enormous challenges and setbacks.

We know that goals can cut through chaos and distraction and bring clarity and focus to our lives.

But knowing your values doesn't automatically make you good at setting goals. You need to deliberately make sure you're setting the kind of goals that are most likely to be reached. SMART goals are a roadmap from where you are to where you want to be:

S is for specific. This cuts down on distractions by definition. Be as clear as possible. Don't just say what will happen, be clear about what you will do, in detail.

M is for measurable. A good goal can be measured or quantified. The outcome is not vague or up for interpretation. Answer the question, "How will I know my goal has been reached?"

A is for attainable. This means it's realistic for you in your situation. A goal should challenge us to move beyond, but it needs to be possible and reasonable.

R is for relevant. Does this goal actually speak to your broader values? Does the smaller goal fit in with the bigger one, and does it make sense in context?

T is for time-bound. Set a deadline for when the goal should be accomplished by, or outline some time limits. Goals set for "someday" never materialize.

Here is an example of a fairly poor goal: "I want to become healthier."

Here is the same goal, written to satisfy each of the SMART criteria: "I want to eat at least five servings of different fruit and vegetables daily (i.e., each serving is eighty grams), in my effort to have a better diet in general, and I want to maintain this every day for the remainder of the month."

Here, the goal is specific (it's five different fruit and veggies a day), measurable (we can track eighty grams), attainable (not very unrealistic), relevant (makes sense for the broader goal of a better diet), and time-bound (both in the short term since it's daily, but in the long term since it carries on until the end of the month).

Now, SMART goals don't change the difficulty of the tasks ahead of you. But they *do* help you shape and define your vision so you can act with more efficiency. They get you thinking more carefully about what you're actually doing and how. So many of us embark on missions with very little idea of the details, and only end up disappointing ourselves as the plan quickly falls apart. With a SMART goal, you are basically plotting a journey from the present to the future, and any activity is bound to be more successful when there's a clear and logical plan for it.

It might feel a little obvious and cheesy to literally write your goals out, but just try it and you may be surprised by how unclear the vision really is. Ask yourself honestly if a vague and diffused goal is actually bringing more stress into your life. Is it possibly inviting pressure and tension without actually giving you a clear feeling of how to resolve that tension?

Tighten your goals up a little (or, if they're completely unattainable, loosen them up!) and you'll discover that a clear, proactive, and appropriate focus on what matters makes you more determined to fulfill your plan—and less stressed.

Kanban Method
Most of these methods share one fundamental principle: the more information you can get out of your head (i.e., the more organized and efficient you are), the less you have to worry about and the less you'll overthink. Kanban is a visual system for managing workflows, but you can use many of its principles to enhance your personal productivity. This is a technique that concerns the actual flow of work and how we can improve it.

The Japanese Kanban method originated in a manufacturing context as a way to organize things like factories for maximum efficiency. Applied to a personal life, Kanban is great for looking at systems and processes that are already underway, and improving them. Note, though, that it cannot help you identify goals or set up systems; rather, it allows you to continually streamline systems already in place.

There are four foundational principles to keep in mind:

1. Start with what you're already doing
2. Make constant, incremental changes for the better
3. Respect current rules and limitations (at least initially)
4. Think about encouraging leadership wherever possible

For our purposes as individuals (and not, say, a Toyota factory), it's the second principle of constant improvement that we're most interested in. The idea is that you actually achieve more by pursuing small, cumulative baby steps rather than trying to make big (intimidating!) quantum leaps. In Kanban, you use six core actions to shape the existing flow, and inch it gradually toward something better and better:

1. Visualize your workflow. Whether this is literally your occupation or some other "work" (writing your novel, exercising), put it up on a board so you see it visually, step by step. Use different colors, symbols, or columns to sort the stages of your process. Remember, the more you can put *out there*, the less you have to worry about *in here*.
2. Avoid works in progress. This is great for "firefighter" or "time martyr" types. Basically, don't multitask. Pick up one thing, give it your full attention, complete the task, then pick up the next. This curbs the temptation to always be thinking about what's next in line (i.e., overthink!). Don't leave unfinished tasks to stress and overwhelm you.

3. Manage the flow. Look to see how your attention, time, and energy is flowing from task to task. Are you losing lots of time to commuting or waiting? Do you switch tasks often and then lose that time where you constantly have to get back in the flow? Look at where you're wasting time and smooth out your process. This could be as simple as noticing that you can get two chores done in one car trip rather than wasting time and fuel on two separate ones.

4. Set up feedback loops. In the business world, this is called "fail fast and fail often," but really what it means is that you need to build in time to consistently check in with how you're doing, adjust, and repeat. Look at your process and your efforts and see if they're actually working (which you can do because you set SMART, measurable goals). With constant feedback loops comes constant improvement.

5. "Improve collaboratively, evolve experimentally." This concept is a little less applicable to ordinary life, but in a non-commercial setting it teaches us to apply the scientific method to everything we do. We can establish a hypothesis, test it, and refine our knowledge by constantly using experiments.

While all this may seem a little abstract for the ordinary person looking to cut down on overthinking, the concepts are sound wherever they're applied. For example, let's say you are constantly stressed by meal prep and grocery shopping and find the never-ending question of what to make for dinner quite stressful. So you sit down and sketch out, visually, the process of food shopping in your home, from buying things at the store to planning meals to cooking (and emergency takeout when there's nothing in the fridge).

Once you visualize it, you identify where the flow isn't working and discover that you're actually throwing away a lot of food while simultaneously running out at the end of the week, thus causing stress. You decide to manage the flow by implementing a new system where you rank food according to its best-by date. You try this for a week and then see if a) your food process improved and b) your stress went down. Knowing that incremental progress is the goal, you make some tweaks and try again.

True, initially it may feel like you're thinking *more* about this problem, but here, your thoughts are not useless rumination that only makes you feel bad; instead, you are empowering yourself to make changes, take charge of your day-to-day life, and find what actually works. Essentially, you build a life around yourself that's perfectly designed to take stress off your mind, not add to it!

Finally, let's look at a clever way to efficiently use the time we've allocated for each task once we've considered how it may fit into a bigger process.

Time Blocking

Most of us spend considerable time every day doing one thing: working. Yet it's so easy to waste time on meetings, emails, and "busy work" that takes your attention away from what counts and encourages overthinking. Time blocking is great for those firefighters, procrastinators, and time martyrs who want to take control of their work schedules to cut stress. It can help you get out of reactive, distracted mode and prevent those days that feel chopped up, interrupted, or chaotic.

With time blocking, you dedicate certain blocks of time in your schedule to one task and that task alone, rather than multitasking or rapidly switching between this and that. By planning ahead, you waste no time or willpower making decisions about what to do, and you can ensure you always begin with your priorities. You want to encourage "deep work" and get engrossed in what you're doing, rather than shallow attention on many things at once. This is not only effective (i.e., you get more done in a fixed space of time) but it's far less stressful, and you may get more out of work with less mental or emotional effort.

Deep work constitutes all those things in your "urgent and important" and "important but not urgent" tasks, whilst shallow work is all that other stuff—the tasks you want to delegate or get rid of entirely. A good day is one in which you spent the most time possible on those tasks that genuinely enrich your life and help reach your goals, while minimizing how much shallow work you have to do and how stressed it can make you. Time blocking can curb the perfectionist impulse and give you a more realistic idea of how long things actually take.

- Start by asking what you hope to achieve with a day or a week, and what priorities you want to focus on. This will guide your approach.

- Then look at the morning and evening routines you want to establish at the start and end of every single day. For example, you might start with a morning workout and meditation and end with a relaxing read or quality time with family. Of course, these are all set according to your priorities and values (not to mention your unique sleep/wake cycles and habits).

- Next, block in the priority tasks first, planning them for when you know you'll be most alert and energetic. Keep these blocks as undivided as possible.

- Then find room for less important shallow work and schedule for times when you are not as productive.

- Of course, you will need a time every day for those tasks you can't exactly predict, such as responding to emails or other things that emerge in the moment. Set aside some time to address these so they can't build up and stress you out. Having this set time also means you can confidently forget about reactive tasks outside of their designated window.

- Take a look at your schedule and try it out for a few days. It's not gospel—see what works and change what doesn't.

Let's look at an example. Marie is definitely *not* a morning person—she has never understood how anyone can get anything done in the morning, let alone at 5 or 6 a.m.! Instead, over time, she has understood that she is most productive and alert much later in the day – around 1 p.m. She knows that starting at 1 p.m., she gets a strong burst of energy that lasts around two or three hours, so this is when she blocks off time for her most challenging work tasks.

From 8 a.m. to 1 p.m., however, she does all the things that require less energy. She does "life admin" tasks; completes her daily exercise; schedules meetings and chats; and sorts out bills, shopping, and other niggles. She isn't too concerned with the order she does these tasks in, but when 1 p.m. hits, she shuts her door, puts on her headphones, and works solidly for two hours straight, no breaks, no excuses.

After this time block, she starts to lose energy again. This is where she finishes up any last-minute tasks, but they are the kind of thing where it won't matter too much if she has to postpone to some other time. The rest of the evening she relaxes and then sleeps. She knows that socializing late into the night completely throws her schedule, so to coincide with her natural energy peak, she makes sure to plan to see friends and do outings on weekends. She also knows to gently shift the pattern an hour or two in the winter, when things are darker and colder.

At first, while trying this schedule, Marie feels a little guilty—like she's shirking her work responsibilities. In actual fact, her routine is both less stressful *and* more effective. Work that would take four and a half hours when scheduled at an awkward, easily interrupted time of day takes only two hours to do when attempted during the energy peak, for example. What's worse, that four and a half hours may bring four and a half hours of stress into Marie's life, whereas the two focused, intense hours are barely felt at all.

When people apply time-blocking rules to their real lives, they are often surprised to discover that **the thing that makes life stressful is somehow also the thing that makes it more productive**!

Many people schedule deliberate rest and leisure times and make sure there's a little buffer between each task just in case. You might also like to have a day in the week dedicated to catch-up or for "overflow" so you don't feel like it's all or nothing.

Remember—your schedule is there to help you be in control; it's not in control of *you*. If something doesn't work, tweak it. Try out different schedule-managing apps, calendars, or reminders. Try longer or shorter blocks, and even build in a period every day where you stop and appraise how you did and why. In time, your schedule could become one of your most powerful stress-reduction tools—not to mention it can make you far, far more productive.

Takeaways

- One of the biggest sources of our anxiety is poor time management. We tend to prioritize things that make us miserable and refuse to give enough time to things we really enjoy. We seldom take time out for adequate leisure and relaxation, so we must consciously do this in order to improve our anxiety levels. Some tips to follow are making regular to-do lists, prioritizing your tasks in the order of your actual preference, and breaking goals down into smaller pieces.

- There are also other strategies that can help us manage our time better. One of these is called Allen's input processing method. Here, inputs are any external stimulus. What we need to do is analyze and take note of how we respond to even the most minute stimulus, like calls, emails, etc. Then, we must plan for the best way to respond based on our existing responses so that we can prioritize certain stimuli over others.

- Another useful technique is to use SMART goals. This stands for specific, measurable, attainable, relevant, time-bound goals. Note your goals down in very specific detail so you know exactly what to do. Then, set up criteria for measuring how you'll know you've achieved this goal. Make sure that the goal is attainable; it shouldn't be something outlandish. Assess how this goal is relevant to your value system and what purpose achieving it will fulfill in your life. Lastly, set a time limit for completing this goal so that you do it in a reasonable amount of time.

Chapter 4. How to Find Instant Zen

If you make the effort to structure and organize your time according to your values and goals, you will naturally find that your stress levels become more manageable, and overthinking ebbs a little. In the space where your mind used to be filled with anxious over-rumination, you can start to breathe a little and think about the conscious actions you'd like to take according to what matters to you.

Nevertheless, you can't plan for everything in life, and there's no way around the fact that unexpected events can and do happen. Sometimes you can get caught in the grip of anxious overthinking despite the best-laid plans.

In this chapter, we'll look at practical in-the-moment ways to reduce anxiety once it's already threatening to take over. The techniques we'll discuss can be used both as a kind of daily preventative and as an immediate remedy in the moment. But one thing is clear: relaxation is something to practice just the same as any other good habit. We cannot rely on relaxation to just happen by itself. And there's no reason to reserve these techniques for situations that have already gone south—rather, we can do them anytime.

When you relax, your heart rate, breathing, and blood pressure drop; your digestion and blood sugar levels improve; you moderate stress hormones in the body; you reduce fatigue and muscle pain; and you increase concentration, good sleep, and confidence. And all this spells less anxiety and rumination. Combined with other techniques in this book, relaxation is a powerful tool for mitigating the stress of living.

We'll consider three main techniques here: **autogenic relaxation, progressive muscle relaxation, and visualization.** Much like the 5-4-3-2-1 technique, these three all work because they encourage your mind to settle into calm focus and awareness of the body in the moment, and not on the storm of thoughts in your mind. These practices can be done more formally with a professional, or you can schedule some time every day to practice them at home. Once you're familiar with them, however, you have an inventory of stress management techniques you can pull out whenever necessary.

Autogenic Training

From "auto" meaning self and "genetos" meaning born or originating, autogenic relaxation is relaxation that comes from within you. Combining visual imagery, breathing, and awareness of your body, you work to calm yourself. In a sense, all the techniques in this book are autogenic because they rely on your ability to move yourself from a stressed state to one of relative calm and work with the body's innate anti-stress mechanisms.

This kind of approach was proposed by Johannes Schultz in the 1920s, who also had an interest in hypnosis and other forms of deep relaxation. Autogenic training was intended to systematically induce these calm states of body and mind at will—excellent for those suffering from anxiety. A study in the journal *Asian Nursing Research* found that subjective stress response was greatly improved when nurses received autogenic training. Meanwhile, more recent research in 2021 by Rivera and colleagues in the journal *Frontiers in Psychology* found that autogenic training had demonstrable effects on stress management during the Covid-19 pandemic in Spain.

Today there are autogenic training centers all over the world (with most in the UK, Japan, and Germany) working from Schultz's research, and you can also pursue training of this kind through a certified psychotherapist. But you don't need to do any formal training or conduct research studies to understand the basic principles for yourself. It's all about deliberately calming the central nervous system, which is where anxiety and overthinking begin, biologically speaking. Instead of being reactive and helpless in the face of distressing thoughts and sensations, you learn to control and direct them, regulating your own emotional state *and* your physiological arousal.

There are six main techniques spanning the entire body and mind, and formal sessions last around twenty minutes. The "trainee" may begin in a comfortable position, and the trainer uses verbal cues to guide attention onto awareness of body sensations. For example, the trainer might say, around five or six times, "I am completely calm," followed by, "My right arm is heavy," "I am completely calm," "My left arm is heavy," and so on, moving through the body repeating these cues over and over. This process is then reversed at the end of the session; for example, by using phrases like, "My arm is firmed up," and, "I am alert," to awaken out of the relaxation.

The six techniques or "lessons" use cues that promote awareness of the following:

- Heaviness

- Warmth

- Awareness of heartbeat

- Awareness of breath

- Awareness of abdominal sensations

- Focus on coolness of the forehead

At the end of each session, the trainee has learned not just to relax, but to have better control over their own awareness of stimuli of all kinds. Through practicing these techniques, you develop more empowerment and control over your internal world. In fact, a meta-analysis conducted in *Applied Psychophysiology and Biofeedback* showed evidence for the technique's effectiveness in treating a range of conditions, from hypertension to depression, asthma, migraines, anxiety, phobias, pain, insomnia, and more. There's no reason that regular practice can't help the ordinary stress and tension of daily life and boost self-esteem in the process. Here's a brief guide for how to attempt a session on your own:

1. Find a comfortable position, sitting or lying down, take some slow deep breaths, and begin by slowly repeating to yourself six times, "I am completely calm." If you are doing the second "lesson," for example, you can focus on warmth. Put your awareness onto sensations of warmth in your body.

2. Then repeat, also six times, "My left arm is warm," followed by six repetitions of, "I am completely calm." Say this slowly and really engage with the sensations, slowing

your breath and focusing only on your body.

3. Follow up with your other arm, both legs, chest, and abdomen, alternating with, "I am completely calm."

4. Reverse the process by saying, "Arms, firm up," "I am alert," and so on and finally, "Eyes open," as you end the session. It should take fifteen to twenty minutes in total.

Every time you attempt this process, focus on a different sensation, i.e., heaviness first, then warmth, then heartbeat, and so on through all six. Once you have done this, you can combine them into a single session. For example:

"My arms are heavy."

"My legs are warm."

"My heartbeat is calm and regular."

"My breath is calm and regular."

"My abdomen is relaxed."

"My forehead is pleasantly cool."

Throughout, what's important is that you take your time and really sink into the sensations. Don't rush, and really tune into guiding the desired feeling of calm within you. Feel how your body actually becomes calm when you say, "I am calm." Magic! It's important to stress here that autogenic training does take some time to show the full extent of its benefits. It will require both dedication and commitment to the exercise. However, if you manage to do the hard work, the fruits of your labor will be endless because you'll have mastered the art of controlling your stress levels through a simple exercise that can be done anytime, anywhere. You'll also be able to exercise some control over internal biological processes that are generally beyond the influence of our will, such as heartbeat, body temperature, blood pressure, etc. Take a few minutes out of each day, several times if possible, and try to practice this process regularly. You'll eventually see just how effective this can be to help you stop overthinking.

If you find that this technique appeals, you might like to investigate whether there are professionals or courses available in your area that can help you fine tune the details. You can also discover online tools or audio recordings that will prompt the various stages of the process, making it easier if you're a beginner. Of course, you could also create a simple audio recording yourself—simply record the instructions/prompts with adequate pauses in between, and play them back to yourself every session.

It should be noted that there are some risks associated with trying these techniques on your own and without the guidance of a trained professional. On rare occasions, the techniques might make certain people feel more anxious or depressed. However, those without pronounced mental health concerns can most likely safely attempt a few simple techniques inspired by autogenic training. Moreover, it is not advisable for people to attempt autogenic training if they suffer from diabetes or a heart condition. Some also experience either a sharp increase or decrease in blood pressure as a result of autogenic training. If you have any of these health issues, it is highly advisable to check in with your doctor the next time you pay them a visit and make sure autogenic training is safe for you.

Guided Imagery and Visualization

Without even trying to, you might have done a little visualization when doing autogenic relaxation, perhaps imagining that the warmth you were feeling was like a hazy red glow around your body, or that the heaviness was because your legs were made of lead and were sinking into a soft, fluffy cloud. Mental images like this work to tie together your mental and physical world, bringing your awareness, thoughts, and sensations into alignment in the present moment. This is like taking the same mental machine that ordinarily overthinks and stresses us and steering it toward a destination that calms and balances us instead.

Your brain can go at a thousand miles an hour and imagine anxiety-provoking scenes that have absolutely nothing to do with reality, but your physical body is slower and your senses are almost always going to give you an accurate reading on the environment, provided you tune into them with enough sensitivity. Using visualization helps us to change gears, slow down, and take more control over a runaway brain.

It's not just about visual imagination, though—the more senses involved, the better. Use sight, sound, touch, taste, and smell to paint an image mentally of a soothing "place" that encourages positive feelings. After all, when we overthink, we are already doing the opposite—painting a distressing hypothetical world in painful detail and putting ourselves inside it!

This technique can be done alone, with a professional, or with a recording of spoken cues (more often labeled "guided imagery"). It can be paired with massage, progressive muscle relaxation (we'll explore this shortly), autogenic techniques, or even something like yoga. The idea is a familiar one: if we can conjure up a relaxing scene internally, we can control our own stress response, willing ourselves to feel relaxed instead of letting overthinking and stress unbalance us. It goes a little further than mere distraction because what you are doing is reorienting your awareness to relaxing sensations and away from stressful ones.

Your body and mind work together. If you close your eyes and imagine, with vivid detail, a juicy, sour lemon, your mouth will inevitably start to water even though the lemon isn't real. With this logic, we use our minds to behave as if we were in a calm place and feeling relaxed, and our body follows, not able to distinguish between the scenario and the *thought* of the scenario. If you routinely practice visualization, you are also training yourself with a cue that you can quickly use to access that state of mind again, returning to your "happy place" whenever you want to.

It's a revelation in itself: we are not subject to the whims of our bodies or the random churning of our minds, but can *consciously and deliberately shape our state of mind*—and the more we practice, the more masterful we can be. In meditation, we cultivate awareness and come into the moment; with guided imagery and visualization, we do the same, but once we have detached from stressful thoughts, we then direct our awareness to a target of our choosing. Meditation and visualization can work beautifully together.

The great thing about visualization is that you already have everything you need to start. You can do it anywhere, for as long as you like, and as often as you like. It literally is limited only by your imagination. However, it is something that initially takes some patience and dedication, and while you are getting the hang of it, you need to carve out a space and time where you won't be interrupted or distracted.

Jessica Nguyen and Eric Brymer published research findings in a 2018 paper titled *Nature-Based Guided Imagery as an Intervention for State Anxiety.* They found that imagining peaceful and beautiful scenes from nature had a profound effect on wellbeing and lowered the stress response—even more than imagery that was more urban or neutral. While you don't *have to* imagine serene forests or breath-taking ocean landscapes, the research does seem to suggest that incorporating imagery from the natural world has measurable benefits—plus, it's a great solution for those who find themselves trapped indoors.

The general technique goes as follows:

- Find a comfortable position and relax your breathing; center yourself and close your eyes.

- In as much detail as you can, take your time to imagine a location of your choosing, so long as it makes you feel happy, calm, or energized. You might choose a cool, mystical forest, a beach, a snug blanket beside a fire in a library, or even a beautiful crystal palace on a faraway purple planet (it's your image, you do what you like!).

- As you imagine the details of this place—the way it smells, the colors, the sounds, even how it feels and tastes—also summon up how you want to feel. Perhaps calm and blissed out, perhaps happy and content. Imagine yourself in the place and see yourself smiling or sitting calmly somewhere.

- You might create a little story for yourself— maybe you bathe in a glittering fountain that washes away stress, or you talk to a friendly angel, or you picture yourself gathering up an armful of beautiful flowers. Take your time here and spend at least five or ten minutes in this place.

- Once you feel ready, gently come out of your image, open your eyes, and stretch a little. You might like to include a closing element in the image itself. For example, you can imagine folding up the scene as though it were a painting and putting it in your pocket to access later. Tell yourself that you can always come back here whenever you like.

As with autogenic techniques, you want to focus on your emotional state; try saying things like, "I feel calm and content," or any favorite mantra, or combine your guided imagery with a focus on sensations of warmth and heaviness. For example, you might focus your attention on each of your limbs while in your imagination, picturing all stress and worry as little bubbles that leave you and float away. Or you could pair the sensation of coolness on your forehead with being in a lovely refreshing stream, where you splash the water on your body and focus on how soothing and lovely it feels.

Not only does guided imagery help reduce anxiety levels, but it's also known to help people access wisdom that they hold on a subconscious level. The technique is so simple yet effective that it is increasingly being incorporated as a supplementary form of psychological treatment along with conventional techniques. Even people suffering from serious issues such as post-traumatic stress, abuse, depression, etc., have found that this technique helps reduce stress and make it more manageable.

If you tend to overthink, overanalyze, or get anxious, remind yourself that this technique is more play than work. Forget about what your visualization *should* be—rather, stretch your mental legs and let your imagination have fun with creating a world exactly as you like it.

As we've said, it might take a while to get the hang of. This is mainly because the stories you create yourself need to be sufficiently detailed to be as evocative as they can be for relaxation. You might discover that even though you consider yourself an overthinker, your thoughts in this regard are surprisingly flat and empty and actually lack any vivid color and depth.

If you find yourself having vague, dis-embodied thoughts, try to bring them back into the senses.

Don't just *think* "calm" but really try to *feel* it with your senses in your mind's eye. What color is calm? What texture beneath your fingers? What does it look and smell and sound like? What actions and symbols and stories go along with this concept for you?

The activity can feel slightly awkward and confusing to begin with, and you might struggle to fully immerse yourself in the mental image. To make things easier, some people imagine a "wise guide" with them who does the job of taking you to a relaxing place, instead of you having to do it yourself. Regardless of how you do it, guided imagery is very similar to self-hypnosis in that it helps you reach a deep state of relaxation that will leave you in a much more positive frame of mind than when you started.

Progressive Muscle Relaxation

Finally, let's add one more powerful technique: conscious control and awareness of our muscles. With prolonged stress comes the fight-or-flight response, where the brain alerts the body to release a cascade of neurotransmitters and hormones that prepare the body for action or to flee. One effect these hormones have is to tense the muscles, which is why sufferers of chronic stress can experience aches, pains, muscle tightness, and tension headaches.

Those who suffer from social anxiety disorder are particularly prone to tensing their muscles due to stress—and they may not be aware of it. Remember that the body and the mind are one thing. When you overthink, your brain lights up with electrochemical activity that is then converted to a biological reality in your body via the body's messengers, hormones. These then cause your body to tense up, tighten, and constrict.

Perhaps you've noticed that you're an overthinker, but what does that actually look like, reflected in your tissues and organs? Or in your GI tract? When we stress, our entire body responds—stress is not just something that happens inside our skulls. Overthinkers can be somewhat disconnected from their bodies and, for example, never notice that their chronic shoulder pain or teeth-grinding and their anxiety are actually one and the same problem. The brain is tense, and so then are the muscles of the body.

But it gets more interesting. A 2017 study published in *Chronic Stress* was titled, "Chronic pain and chronic stress: two sides of the same coin?" The research findings suggested that both muscle pain and chronic stress shared a root cause of being unable to moderate negative thoughts, emotions, and memories, therefore disrupting overall equilibrium. On closer inspection, PTSD, depression, and ongoing muscle pain were seen as separate symptoms of one larger condition mediated by the HPA axis. Stress can make us literally tighten our muscles, causing pain, but it can also interfere with our subjective *perception* of pain.

We can relieve both kinds of tension and dysregulation with progressive muscle relaxation.

Besides relieving muscle tension, there are other benefits to progressive muscle relaxation, though—better digestive health (there is a strong link between mental tension and muscular spasm in the GI tract) and lower blood pressure.

Progressive muscle relaxation is taking control of your muscles to deliberately loosen and relax them, as well as heighten your awareness of these sensations and your degree of control over them. Doctors have long observed that a muscle, when tightened strongly then released, tends to release tension and be more relaxed than before it was tightened. It may seem counterintuitive, but you can achieve deeper states of muscular relaxation when you begin with tensing first, as opposed to just attempting to relax a muscle that's already stressed.

Edmund Jacobson suggested in the 1930s that if one is physically relaxed, one can't help but be *mentally* relaxed, too. He proposed muscle relaxation techniques to try for around ten or twenty minutes daily. This practice can easily be added onto a meditation routine, or at the end or beginning of exercise, or you can do it as part of your winding down routine every evening before bed, perhaps paired with some visualization, journaling, gentle reading, or even prayer or music.

The technique is simple:

- While in a comfortable position, preferably with eyes closed, move your focus from one body part to the next, first tensing the muscle as tightly as possible, then releasing that tension completely before moving on to the next body part.

- Begin with the furthest extremities, like fingers and toes, then move inward so you finish with your abdomen and chest, then finally the small muscles of your face and the surface of your scalp. You can also start with your head and work your way downward if that suits you better.

- Inhale and contract the muscle as hard as you can for a count of five or ten; exhale fully as you let go completely and suddenly. Notice any differences in the sensations in the muscle (a little guided imagery can help—imagine squeezing tension out of your muscles like a sponge).

- Finish with a few deep breaths and a stretch; notice how you feel. This technique not only helps you relax physically, but also improves your body awareness, teaching you to pay closer attention to where stress is accumulating in your body. You may even find with time that your intuition about your overall health is improved as you "read" your body more closely.

You need to tense different parts of your body in different ways. While areas like your biceps, upper arms, hands, and thighs can be clenched, areas like your shoulders need to be shrugged by raising them sharply toward your ears. Your forehead can be wrinkled into a deep frown, while your eyes should be shut tightly together. Next, to tense your jaws and facial muscles, you need to smile as widely as you can. Your stomach will become tense if you suck it into a tight knot, whereas your back needs to be arched sharply. This might feel like a lot to remember, but once you try it a few times, you'll start intuitively making the muscles tense accordingly.

Practicing progressive muscle relaxation regularly has a number of benefits besides just reducing your anxiety levels. It can improve the quality of your sleep, ease neck and lower back pain, decrease the frequency of migraines, and prevent other health issues as well.

Autogenic training, visualization, and muscle relaxation are all, in a way, variations of the same theme: you want to learn to take control of where your conscious awareness is settling and guide it toward your body, the present moment, and the input from your five senses, and away from stressful rumination and overthinking. Mental and emotional mastery comes from gradually learning that *you are in control*, not just of your thoughts but of your emotions and your physical body, too.

Worry Postponement

One final (and amazingly simple) technique for putting the brakes on the anxiety and worry spiral is called worry postponement. In fact, you don't even need to suffer from anxiety to benefit from using it—it's a great all-around stress management technique. A little like making a stress budget.

A randomized trial led by Anke Versluis at the University of Leiden supported the idea that you don't need to completely vanquish worry—but simply make an agreement with yourself to not do it right away. Their research focused on people's tendency to report "subjective health complaints," but the idea can be applied to many other measures of anxiety and rumination. According to their findings, worry postponement is an effective way to put objective distance between a person and their distressing thoughts, as well as practice a degree of metacognition, which can reduce overall anxiety and overthinking.

Again, we see the difference between anxious pushing away, avoiding, and fighting against stress-inducing thoughts versus calmly mastering them and facing them head-on with awareness.

Anxious and worried thoughts are kind of sticky. They have an intrusive quality. Once a threatening or negative thought pops into your head, it seems hard to shift or ignore. You can quickly get distracted since your brain thinks, "Oh, here's what I *really* should be paying attention to!" and just like that, your attention and focus is pulled away from the present moment.

So, what's really happening is that worries are controlling you rather than you controlling them. A stressful thought comes along and cracks the whip, and you instantly obey. The mistake we make is to think that if a negative thought comes along, there is no other option but to focus on it. Remember our brain's negativity bias and our information-processing software that literally evolved to amplify bad news? It tells us that the threatening and scary thing always takes precedence.

Now, if the worry is, "I wonder whether that tiger in front of me is going to try to eat me," then obviously, prioritize that. But usually the worry is something like, "I wonder if Jenny thinks my presentation sucks," or, "What if identity thieves have gone through my trash and discovered that journal I threw out by accident, and now everyone at the FBI knows my terrible secrets?" In other words, we give these thoughts priority when we really, really shouldn't.

Worry postponement isn't saying you're going to completely eradicate worries (yes, we all have them, even non-anxious people). It's just saying you're going to put worries in their proper place. This instantly puts *you* into a proactive state of control. Rather than jumping to attention every time some anxious idea pops into your head, you make it wait. *You* are in charge of where your conscious awareness goes. You don't allow just anything to distract you or disrupt your focus.

Worry postponement is exactly what it sounds like—a deliberate choice to *put off* worrying for another time. This is different from saying you won't worry. Because you will. This is more about taking control and managing your worry, proactively deciding how much of an impact you want it to have on your life. In the moment, worry can seem so urgent and all-important. It can seem non-negotiable that you turn every fiber of your being toward those thoughts and feelings. But actually, you have a choice.

Some studies have found that it is in fact our negative *perception* of our own worry, and not the worry itself, that leads to anxiety. In the 2010 edition of *The Journal of Experimental Psychology*,

Adrian Wells explains how "meta-worry," or the negative appraisal of ordinary worry, can actually lead to more serious generalized anxiety disorders. Thus, when we pathologize and resist our own worry, we essentially entrench it and make it more of a problem than it is. Worry postponement gets around this by saying, "It's not a problem. You can worry all you like, and it's not forbidden. Except you can't do it *now*." This alone can have the effect of dissolving both worry and meta-worry (i.e., worry about worry).

Worry postponement can be done in a few different ways, but it's all about setting deliberate and conscious limits to worry. Like drawing a little fence around it.

One method is to limit the time period when you worry. For example, you get into bed at night and prepare to sleep, but your brain instantly switches into worry mode and brings up a thousand things it wants to stew over. You tell yourself, "That's fine. I'm allowed to worry about that, and I will. But I won't do it *now*. I'll schedule a specific time to worry about this later. Let's say, tomorrow at 10:00 a.m. Before that period, I won't spend a single second thinking about any of this."

And then you do that. If your mind wanders over to those ultra-important, life-or-death thoughts, you can confidently tell yourself that it's fine, you'll think about it, just not now. Chances are, the worries are not all that time sensitive and can wait. In fact, you'll be fresher in the morning and can bring your full brain to the task, if you even still want to. Tell yourself you have already done everything you need to do, the worrying is ticked off the list, and there is nothing outstanding for you to do right now. Just sleep.

An alternative is to put limits on the duration of worry. So, you get up in your bed and tell yourself, "Right, you want to worry? Okay, let's worry. But we are only doing this for *five minutes*, and then we're going to sleep." Set a timer, worry your heart out, and then stop. You may notice a few things with either of these techniques.

The first is that if you delay the worry, you often don't want to do it later anyway. The second is that even when you do permit yourself some worry time, you'll often notice that your anxiety levels are exactly the same before the worry and after. Meaning, the worry time did precisely zero to help. In either case, you are limiting and managing the effect that worry has on you and teaching yourself that you have a choice and are not at the mercy of distracting, intrusive thoughts.

To practice this technique needs preparation and practice. Set a time every day when you purposefully worry. Pick a time when you won't be disturbed and when you're likely to be in your best frame of mind. Experiment a little and don't be afraid to try a few different things before it feels right.

I hear what you're thinking, though. Maybe you're wondering, "Sure, sounds good, but what if this time I really *do* need to worry about something? What if this time it's serious?" Worry will come up with some creative and novel ways to capture your attention, and the nature of worry is such that you can convince yourself that if you stop stressing this one time, calamity really will strike.

Well, let's play devil's advocate and imagine that occasionally, our worries and fears and ruminations actually are very important and need to be considered immediately. What we need is a method for distinguishing between those situations and simple overthinking. We can ask ourselves the question: **is this worry a 1) genuine problem that 2) I can do something about right now?**

Be honest. The problem has to be both objectively critical but also actionable in that very moment. Let's say there's a pressing work matter that's eating you up inside. It is indeed a real problem, but let's say it's late at night and the one person you need to speak to is unavailable until morning. So, the problem is genuine but you cannot do anything about it now. Let's say your child has a fever but is otherwise fine, but you could possibly rush them to the emergency room to be looked at. This is a problem that can be acted on, but it isn't that genuine a problem. Finally, imagine you're worried a recent client is going to leave you a bad review. In reality, this is not really a serious problem (no business ever failed on the back of a single bad review), *and* there's nothing you can do about it right now.

But what if it is a serious problem and you can act right now? Then act.

But act—don't worry. Worry and overthinking are useless, particularly when appropriate action is what's called for. Here, you need to worry even less, since having a calm, clear mind is what will help you see the solution most quickly. Unless your anxious thought is genuinely serious and you can do something sensible in the moment, postpone it. Make the call in the morning, sort it out later, or just drop it for the time being.

Once you've decided that something is not worth worrying about, be ruthless. Imagine your mind is a dog on a leash and keep pulling it back to the present. This is easiest to do if you engage all five of your senses to anchor you in the real, present moment. Examine your environment to see if you can list three sights, three sounds, three smells, and so on.

When worry time comes, notice if the urgency seems diminished somehow. Remind yourself that what once seemed urgent doesn't stay that way. Look with fresh eyes on concerns and anxieties. Go into problem-solving mode and see if committing to taking useful action reduces your anxiety. Sometimes, the best thing you can do for a worry is to pull it into the real world, make it a practical problem, then act on it.

Takeaways

- There may be times when you feel that your anxiety is reaching a fever pitch or that it's on the verge of spiraling out of your control. In such cases, you can rely on some tried and tested techniques to reduce your stress levels.
- The first of these techniques is autogenic training. Through this, we aim to gain control over our thoughts and emotions through six different exercises. To practice the first technique, find a comfortable place to sit or lie down. Then, give yourself certain verbal cues like, "I am completely calm," while breathing slowly and steadily. Feel the sensations in various parts of your body as you intermittently repeat the phrase to yourself. Though this technique might take some time to master, it's simple and can be done anywhere, anytime.
- The second technique is called guided imagery. Essentially, you find a comfortable position and think of a place which engages all your different senses like smell, sound, etc., in pleasantly stimulating ways. This can be any place; it just needs to be one that inspires relaxation. Picture it in as much detail as you can by making full use of your imagination.
- Third, we have progressive muscle relaxation. This technique relies on the theory that physical relaxation leads to mental relaxation.

So, the goal is to physically relax your muscles by first tensing them up. Again, sit in a comfortable position and go from head to toe or vice versa and tense different parts of your body before relaxing and moving on.

- Finally, worry postponement is a very direct and effective way of interrupting anxiety spirals. When you recognize yourself beginning to feel anxious, deliberately schedule a discrete time in the future to worry instead, and then continually bring your mind to the present. We can seldom eliminate worry from our lives, but we *can* consciously limit its time of onset and the duration.

Chapter 5. Rewire Your Thought Patterns

In previous chapters, we've laid a foundation for understanding and fixing overthinking from the inside out. Genuine stress management, taking charge of our mental models and attitudes, building more relaxation into life, and being proactive with how we use our time are all foolproof ways of getting a handle on anxious overthinking. Now, in this chapter, we turn to the thoughts themselves.

Mind, body, and emotions are all connected and mutually influence one another. But you've probably noticed that when it comes to anxiety, the mind plays the most significant role. It's the way we think, our mental structures, and our inner cognitive interpretation of the world that most shapes our experience of it. Understanding this, cognitive behavioral therapy, or CBT, attempts to get to the root of our mind's perception of the world and allows people to generate more helpful, adaptive thoughts.

In an enormous 2018 meta-analysis published in the journal *Depression and Anxiety*, Joseph Carpenter and associates found that CBT tended to relieve anxiety across the board (although results vary with the type of anxiety being treated). A 2019 paper by Colette Hirsch et. al. in *Frontiers in Psychiatry* found that a high seventy four percent of anxious participants experienced recovery after a CBT program. But what about the remaining twenty-six percent?

We address this aspect of the overthinking problem this late in our book because, to be frank, CBT techniques *will not help* if we do not have an adequate grasp on the ideas covered in the previous chapters. Many people find this out the hard way. They realize their overthinking is a problem, so they tackle the issue on the mental and cognitive level. They ignore their excessive caffeine intake, their hectic lifestyles, their unresolved traumas, and their chronic habit of under sleeping. With the best intentions in the world, they embark on a CBT program that then promptly falls apart the second they hit a rough patch or are triggered into an old spiral.

Thoughts emerge from the electrochemical functioning of our brains—and our brains are organs and part of our physical bodies. "Higher order" interventions that attempt to fix overthinking from the top down need to be matched by bottom-up interventions that recognize that thinking is an expression of our biological functioning. In other words, working at the level of thoughts alone is unlikely to be effective unless you also consider all the other aspects of the overthinking puzzle.

That said, negative thought patterns are behind almost all overthinking. Usually, it's not just the *quantity* of thoughts racing around your head, but their *quality*. After all, many people are extremely perceptive and think a lot without it necessarily causing them any distress! With CBT, however, you can get to the root of distorted thoughts and build better ones, i.e., those that help you move through the world with more calm and a sense of control—without medication.

Buckminster Fuller, though not a psychologist, nevertheless showed his understanding of the principles of CBT when he said, "You never change things by fighting the existing reality. To change something, build a new model that makes the existing model obsolete." When we ruminate and overthink, we try to change reality (or worry about changing it), but when we use CBT techniques, what we change is the model itself, or our ways of perceiving.

CBT is used for diagnosed anxiety disorders like panic disorder, OCD, or generalized anxiety, but we can use some of the same techniques ourselves to get a handle on everyday stress, particularly if the source of that stress is our own thoughts.

This is the underlying premise of CBT: our thoughts (not the outside world) influence how we see the world and how we behave. Thoughts create emotions, which shape our perception and change our beliefs about ourselves and how we act. When we change our thoughts, everything else follows. With overthinking, for example, a root thought might be: "Any failure is unbearable, and I'm a bad person if I fail," which means that when you fail, you'll feel awful and may change your behavior so you never risk failing again. However, if your thought is instead: "Failure is normal, and it's not the end of the world," then when you fail, you feel a bit disappointed, but you pick yourself up and carry on.

Better yet, if your thought is, "I value failure as a way to learn more and grow stronger," then when you fail, you feel empowered and motivated and try even harder next time. It's the *same failure* each time, but the thoughts behind it are different, and so the emotions and the resulting behavior are also different. So, it's worth getting to the root of these thoughts, beliefs, and expectations and asking whether they lead to the kind of emotions and behaviors you actually want. If not, they can be changed.

In the following sections, we'll look at how to **identify** thoughts that are not working for you, **challenge** them, and then **restructure** them or **replace** them with thoughts that are more helpful and accurate. Learning this process is essentially a coping skill, which teaches you not only to understand your anxiety on a deep level, but to face and work through those fears rather than let them control you. Think of this as the more proper use of your incredible cognitive powers—instead of anxiously overthinking in circles, you can use your capacity for analysis, conscious thought, and focus to actively improve those parts of your life that aren't working for you.

Unraveling Your Cognitive Distortions

Let's begin with the process of identifying harmful thoughts and beliefs, also called cognitive distortions. Maybe you've never thought about it before, but how *accurate* are your thoughts about the world? We don't see the filter we pass reality through, but in truth, we all view the world through our own personalized set of expectations, beliefs, values, attitudes, biases, assumptions, or flat-out illusions. A big problem for overthinkers is the tendency to take our own word for it! We simply take our appraisals, assumptions, and expectations at face value and act as though they are cold hard fact, completely ignoring the step where we added in our own interpretation. What are your most common cognitive distortions? (Yes, you *do* have them, like all of us!)

See if you can recognize some of your ideas and beliefs in these common types of cognitive distortion:

All-or-nothing thinking. This is overly simplistic, black-and-white thinking. Either someone is completely wrong, or he's completely right, no gray area in between. This is an emotional state stemming from our fight-or-flight response, and you'll recognize it in absolutist language like *never*, *always*, *absolutely*, *completely*, or *nothing*. But this kind of thinking cuts down on compromise, creativity, or nuance. It's associated with helplessness, depression, and inflexibility. When a politician says, "You're with us or you're against us," or your brain tells you, "Get this right or everything will be ruined forever," you are hearing all-or-nothing thinking.

Overgeneralization. This is related to all-or-nothing thinking, where we make sweeping, all-encompassing statements using very little data; for example, "All men are like this," or, "This happens all the time," when in reality, only one man was like that, and the thing happened literally once. This thinking, understandably, raises the stakes, ups anxiety, and makes perfectionistic feelings more pronounced. In fact, 2017 research by Kuru et. al. found a predictable pattern of cognitive distortions in those suffering from social anxiety—and one of the most recognizable patterns was overgeneralization.

Personalization. This was another distortion common to those who tended to have maladaptive appraisals of social situations, and therefore anxiety. When we personalize, we "take things personally." We assume that we are to blame for situations that are in reality outside our control, or assume some meaningful connection between random events and who we are as a person.

For example, someone bumps into us at a bar and spills their drink on our clothes, and we assume that this happened to us and nobody else specifically because that person must have a vendetta against us. We might see a close friend in an awfully bad mood and immediately assume that we are the cause despite any evidence, or we might think that our child doing badly in school means we're terrible parents. As you can imagine, this distortion is responsible for creating anxiety and worry out of thin air!

Internalizing or externalizing. How do we explain certain external events? If we mistakenly assume that we are the reason behind phenomena, we are internalizing. For example, "Mommy and Daddy got divorced because I didn't clean my room enough." Self-blame and low self-esteem are the result, and our overthinking may take a self-reprimanding flavor. Externalizing is going too far the other way and blaming others for what is rightly ours. For example, "It's not my fault she's upset by what I said; she shouldn't be so sensitive." Both these distortions remove agency and lead to a sense of helplessness.

Favoring the negative, discounting the positive. This one is common; we might fail one test in a hundred, but when we say, "I failed," we ignore the other ninety-nine. Perhaps we see success as a lucky chance or fluke, whereas a genuine accident is proof that we are bad, or that bad things *always* happen. This bias speaks to our core beliefs that things will always be bad to such an extent that we don't even see the good anymore.

Emotional reasoning. In this cognitive distortion, we assume that if we feel something is a certain way, we automatically assume that our feelings must point to the truth of that thing. In other words, "If I feel it, it must be true." Say you have a performance review coming up at your job and you have a sneaking suspicion that it won't be very flattering. Though you don't really know how it's going to pan out, you assume that your suspicions have merit and become convinced that a poor review might lead to problems and lower your self-esteem before you've even gotten to know the truth.

These are not the only distortions, but they are some of the most common. Others include catastrophizing ("the only thing that could possibly happen is the worst thing!"), magical thinking ("maybe that crow outside is a sign I shouldn't go out today"), mind reading ("he hates me, I just know it"), fortune telling ("XYZ will happen, I just know it"), or outdated thinking (someone with two PhDs still behaving as though they were an ignorant five-year-old).

Many of us engage in multiple forms of cognitive distortions simultaneously. For example, if we're afraid that a partner has been unfaithful, we might automatically assume that they have in fact cheated (emotional reasoning) and think that it must be because of our own shortcomings (internalization). This can be followed by catastrophizing or fortune telling, wherein you overthink about the consequences of breaking up and ending up single again. The trick is to notice yourself engaging in this thinking in the moment. Look out for strong, emotive language, for words like "should" or "must," for untested assumptions, or for any effort on your part to explain or justify something that, on second look, isn't necessarily the case. Let's look at how to catch these distortions in the wild.

The Antecedent Behavior Consequence Model (ABC)

In the 1970s, Edward Carr and colleagues conducted research that discovered that many problem behaviors were logically linked to a small set of antecedents and consequences. Though their focus was on applied behavioral analysis, the model has been subsequently used to help frame the process of individual behavior change—in our case, the behavior is overthinking, rumination, and worry. The model below can help you understand and identify your own cognitive distortions by looking closely at what comes before (antecedent) and after a behavior (consequence) inspired by a particular thought process. The ABC model focuses primarily on actions and behaviors, but as we've seen, our actions are driven by our thoughts and beliefs.

The **antecedent** is a trigger that cues a behavior. For example, every time you're on the beach, you get an ice cream, and every time your partner is late, you get angry and do the silent treatment. An antecedent can be a person, a word, an environment, a feeling, a situation, a time of day, or a combination of these things.

The **behavior** is the act resulting from the trigger and can be helpful or not so helpful. If you reach for a drink every time you're stressed at work, to the point of alcoholism, then obviously this is not helpful. Some actions are adaptive and help us cope, while others undermine our productivity, make us feel worse, or even put us in danger.

The **consequence** is the outcome, good or bad, of the behavior. Some behaviors improve a situation or make us feel good; others are unhealthy and unhelpful. Typically, we judge actions as good because their consequences are good, and vice versa.

The point of outlining these three parts is to realize that they are actually connected. Sometimes, we don't see how our thoughts influence our behavior and how this behavior concretely affects our lives. Sometimes, we don't see what is really triggering our behavior in the first place, but once we do, we can take steps to avoid or change the trigger, rather than work directly on the behavior itself.

Can you stop and take a look at the causes and effects of certain behaviors? Can you gain insight into why you do as you do, and whether it leads to desirable consequences? Initially, you may need to gather data on your own behavior like a scientist does and look for patterns. Draw up a spreadsheet with four columns and list events so you can tease out the A, B, and C. Gather data for a week or two or until you start to notice recurring patterns. For example:

	Antecedent	Behavior	Consequence
Event 1	Being at the grocery store around lunchtime	Picking up a box of donuts and scoffing them all in the car	Feeling physically sick and ashamed
Event 2	Colleague's birthday at the office	Scoffed a load of cake	Feeling physically sick and ashamed
Event 3	Feeling low after argument with kids	Raided the cupboards for cookies, ate half a box	Felt out of control

In this overly simplified example, someone might quickly come to the realization that they don't overeat because they are an awful, greedy person (in fact, this feeling is actually the *consequence* of overeating) but that they overeat to deal with stress or because environmental cues are triggering associations and learned behavior (i.e., office party = cake time!).

This simple log reveals a few things: that the behavior is actually not working, because the consequence is always negative. It also immediately suggests a way forward: moderate the triggers to avoid the behavior.

Though useful, the technique is better suited to more simple behaviors; you might need the help of a professional to unravel more complex or mysterious tendencies, especially if you're introducing some bias or mistaken ideas into the analysis itself. There are two parts to using the ABC model: first, you gather data to find more insight into existing behaviors, and second, you work to restructure triggers and consequences in an effort to address unwanted behaviors.

Behavior change is possible, but it takes time. It usually works best when you take the global view, i.e., not only consider the architecture surrounding your behavior, but also the thoughts that support that behavior. When it comes to overthinking, we can tie in the ABC method by considering specifically what thoughts precede, accompany, and follow our action, and how our thoughts inform those actions.

There might be plenty of rewarding consequences that inadvertently cement bad behavior (for example, whenever you drink too much, you become the life and soul of the party and get a lot of positive validation from your friends). Looking closely, you can start to unravel not just the behavior, but the thoughts behind it. "If I drink, people like me, so that means if I don't drink, people won't like me as much." You could go cold turkey with mixed success, but you'd probably tackle the anxiety around this drinking problem better if you acknowledged the core beliefs and thoughts that keep the drinking behavior in place.

Keep a Dysfunctional Thought Record

Another way to reduce overthinking and anxiety is to work directly with maladaptive thoughts, especially those behind behaviors that have consequences you don't want in your life. A "dysfunctional thought record" is a structured way to gather all those automatic, even unconscious thoughts in one place so we can analyze them and decide if an alternative would serve us better.

In the same way as we constructed an ABC spreadsheet above, construct a thought record:

Date and time	Situation	Automatic thoughts	Emotions	Alternative response	Outcome

Make an entry in this record every time you experience a strong negative emotion. The record will help you do a "postmortem" on thoughts and feelings and find out what was going on in your mind at the time—useful if you want to make insightful, data-driven changes.

Situation: Record any triggering event or environment that comes before certain thoughts and feelings, much as you did for the "antecedents." This could be a memory, thought, emotion, idea, or little daydream that made you feel a certain way.

Automatic thoughts: Put down the resulting thoughts or images, as well as your degree of belief or investment in them.

Emotions: Tease out the emotion that these automatic thoughts inspired, as well as their intensity as a percentage.

Alternative response: Here, after the initial event has passed, think about the cognitive distortions you might have made, and whether you could have had a different, healthier response. We'll cover this column more fully in the next section about challenging and overcoming these distortions.

Outcome: Fill this in after you've identified and reworked the original thoughts and feelings. Re-evaluate how you feel, how much you believe the automatic thoughts, the intensity of your feelings, and how you want to act.

You can also make an additional column for cognitive distortions. This will help you recognize them more easily over time and observe which distortions you are particularly prone to indulging in. When you make your entries depends on you—but try to note down negative emotions as close to their occurrence as possible.

For example, you might suddenly notice a drastic drop in your mood. You pause and become aware of it, then bring out your thought record. What was the situation? You noted that it was 1 p.m., around lunchtime at home. You can't see why this should trigger a negative emotion until you dig a little deeper and realize that the thought, "It's lunchtime," immediately led to the thought, "But don't eat too much like you always do because you're gaining weight."

This situation and resulting thought led to a subtle but definite cascade of negative feelings. You were not even aware that you were thinking these things at all until you slowed down and took a closer look! The automatic thoughts emerge: "No matter how little you eat, you'll always gain weight and get fatter and fatter, and there's nothing you can do about it!" Examining your thoughts, you see that despite it being invisible to you, you actually believe this thought fully. That's why, in the emotion column, you can put "frustration," "apathy," and "self-pity." Who wouldn't feel that way if they believed that nothing they did could positively influence their lives?

To examine the alternative responses, you first become curious about any cognitive distortions you've made: all-or-nothing, black-and-white thinking and emotional reasoning, with a heavy dose of catastrophizing and discounting the negative.

To counteract these, you change the thought slightly into: "Eating in a healthy way may take effort, but I am always in control of my diet, and I can always improve."

Now, the next time you find yourself in a bad mood around lunchtime, you are not ignorant of the cause, and you do not allow that original distorted thought to carry you along, spawning more and more anxious and negative thoughts as it goes. Rather, you stop it in its tracks and ask if you'd like to give the alternative thought some airtime instead.

This activity is especially useful when you combine it with action. If you had not explored your negative feeling in your thought record, it may have been there all the same, influencing your behavior. You may have felt fatalistic and resentful about it, and decided to binge for lunch—why not, if it's impossible to lose weight anyway? On the other hand, if you're aware of the trigger and have a healthier alternative at hand, you can use this to inspire a different choice. How do you behave when you believe, "I am always in control of my diet, and I can always improve"? Chances are, you make healthier, more conscious choices.

Both the ABC format and the dysfunctional thought record above essentially perform the same function; however, one focuses on behaviors and the other more on the thoughts and feelings behind them. You can use either depending on your unique situation, or try both together to get a richer insight into what's happening internally when you overthink and experience anxiety. Whatever you decide, after a few weeks, you should have gathered sufficient data to move on to the next step: challenging and changing your thoughts.

Getting Rid of Cognitive Distortions

Whichever method you use to challenge your unhelpful thoughts, the idea is always to take control of thought patterns that are making you anxious, and consciously replace them with ways of thinking that help you feel calm, in control, and capable. Again, it's worth remembering to adopt an attitude of compassionate curiosity rather than judgment. People who are anxious or overthinking are often very hard on themselves or beat themselves up for their perceived flaws and weaknesses. If you have noticed patterns in your own cognition and can see some less-than-flattering distortions, then this is a reason to celebrate. Be proud of yourself for having the honesty and courage to grow and change, rather than trying to "fix" yourself from a position of desperation, shame, or impatience. The idea is that we uncover our thoughts so that we can more consciously replace them with ones that better reflect our real values and help us create the life we want for ourselves. It's an empowering process. Let's look at some popular approaches.

Cognitive Restructuring
Isn't it funny how often and how easily we just assume everything we're thinking is completely correct? Most of the time, we don't question the thoughts that run through our minds, but if we can stop and look at our thinking closely, we can identify distortions, inaccuracies, and false narratives that keep us trapped in patterns of overthinking and stress. Whether from old habit and convention, or because of trauma, or because we were taught those beliefs by someone else, these narratives have a funny way of bedding down and convincing us that they are not in fact interpretations of reality, but reality itself.

But, we have to be willing to act like scientists and neutrally examine and question our own thinking, looking for evidence rather than letting any old thought run away with us. This clarity becomes like a sword that helps us cleanly cut through our overthinking and surgically remove from the mess the thoughts that are useful and accurate, and leave behind those that are not doing us any good.

Albert Ellis is often credited with being one of the founding fathers of cognitive therapy, and specifically cognitive restructuring, where we become aware of and revise thought patterns that aren't working for us. We have the choice to construct the thoughts we want and can use evidence to restructure limiting or unhelpful thoughts into more rational ones.

A therapist might ask someone to go out and collect hard data to see whether their thoughts, assumptions, attributions, and interpretations are actually supported in reality. The big insight comes when you realize that much of what you take for granted is done with next to no evidence! And if you chose one set of thoughts, it means you can choose another.

How we feel is not because of what happens, but because of how we think about what happens. When we change the way we look at things, we change the way we feel. In fact, if you've done some observations on your own thinking as described in the previous section, your conscious attention is already changing the way you organize yourself mentally. Just by slowing down and paying attention, you are more aware, giving yourself an opportunity for more agency. Simply by identifying our thoughts rather than running along with them unquestioningly, we think more rationally and more clearly, taking a big step toward breaking stressful mental habits.

Let's take things further. When you feel a negative emotion, STOP. Pause and become alert. Write down as much as you can in your record, whichever style you've opted for. Identify the trigger or cue, or at least whatever came directly before the feeling, and note it down. Go into detail if you can: who was present? Where and when did this happen? Literally what happened, in detail (no detail is too small)?

Write down your automatic thoughts, even if they're not too clear in your mind yet. Watch any self-talk, any questions that pop up, any explanations or stories you immediately begin to tell yourself. The tricky thing is that the most stubborn and damaging automatic thoughts are usually the most vague and difficult to articulate—at first. Notice your resulting emotion (it may seem at first that thought and emotion are the same—look carefully and untangle them!) and how intensely you feel it. You may feel more than one.

Once you're used to this, we get to the important part: changing. Attempt to restructure only after you've spent enough time gathering data neutrally—we are often not in the position to start making changes until we have a clear picture of what we're actually altering! Your alternatives will be guided by the kind of distortion you see yourself making. When you're new to the process, you might want to simply generate as many alternatives as possible—it doesn't matter if they're workable, only that you're opening your mind to see that there are, in fact, other ways to think about things. Look for different interpretations. Soften things or be a little more flexible or kinder in your analysis.

Here are some questions to guide this process:

- What evidence do I have that my automatic thought is actually true or not?
- Are there other explanations?
- Have I made an error or assumption?
- What's the worst that could happen—and is that really *that* bad?
- What cognitive distortions am I using and what does the thought look like when I take this distortion away?
- What would I think of a loved one or friend thinking this thought?
- Have I looked at all the facts or just some of them?
- Is my response a genuine one or am I behaving out of habit?
- What other perspectives are there? What might others make of this situation?

- Where did this thought really come from and is that a reliable source?

Jot down as many alternatives as you can, but three at a minimum. Then, consult your chart again. Look at your thoughts and emotions, but in a fresh light. Is anything different now that you've restructured your thinking? If so, notice and appreciate any benefits. The more you can internalize the fact that cognitive restructuring actually improves your life and makes you feel better, the more likely you are to stick with it and reap the benefits!

Let's look at a concrete example. Mike is a chronic overthinker and has been intensely stressed by recurring worries about work, unable to relax due to fears that everything is always on the verge of catastrophe. He keeps a dysfunctional thought record for a few weeks, and here's one of his entries:

Date and time	Situation	Automatic thoughts	Emotions	Alternative response	Outcome

9 July, 10:45	Feeling rushed in the morning, bumping into boss in hallway and unable to answer his question quickly; he laughed	"Others are constantly watching and evaluating me" "I have to appear perfectly in control and correct at all times" "I'm secretly bad at my job and a failure"	Panic (80%) Shame (10%) Feel like I can never relax, feel like an imposter	**Possible distortion: catastrophizing, overinflation, focusing on the negative, mind reading.**	Feel a lot more comfortable and at ease when I restructure the thoughts.

After a few weeks Mike notices a pattern of the same recurring thoughts and the same kind of distortions again and again. He looks at the thoughts and generates some alternatives inspired by the questions listed earlier:

"I don't have much evidence that people are *judging* me, even if they do occasionally notice my work."

"I might exaggerate how closely my boss actually monitors me."

"I might interpret a laugh as being more menacing than it is."

"I have plenty of evidence that my boss is happy with my work."

"Even if I make a small mistake and others see it, it's not really the end of the world, and it's highly unlikely I'll be fired immediately."

"I don't really know what others think of me, and have no evidence that they think badly of me."

. . . and so on.

With these thoughts in place, Mike notices that his panic, which was originally at eighty percent, drops down to about thirty percent. He notices he doesn't feel shame at all when he thinks more positively. The next time distorted thoughts emerge, he STOPS and remembers that he is in control and has options. Does he want to go down the old mental pathways that lead to rumination and stress? Or does he want to choose a more comfortable, realistic thought pattern?

Behavioral Experiments

When you take the above approach, you are essentially sitting down your overactive mind and questioning all those automatic, unconscious, and unhelpful thoughts it creates. You take on the role of a neutral investigator or scientist, getting to the bottom of things. But some of our most cherished assumptions and biases might linger on even after we've checked them for cognitive distortions and looked for alternatives.

For example, you might have the thought, "Everyone hates me." This may be so ingrained in you from childhood or from your habitual sense of your identity that you can never really shake it even when you acknowledge intellectually that "hate" is probably too strong a word. You could argue with yourself, look for alternative interpretations, yet still feel deep down that this belief is true. There is one way, however, that you can get to the root of this idea: *test it.*

Looking at evidence for our thoughts can go a long way, but sometimes we need to perform "experiments" to prove to ourselves that our thoughts are not founded in reality. Stubborn core beliefs have an emotional component, which means they won't simply disappear because you've rationally argued them away. So, try this technique instead:

- **Clarify the belief**. State clearly what your thought is and write it down, as well as the associated emotion and its intensity. In this example, "Everyone hates me."
- **Create a hypothesis**, which contains a potential alternative, i.e., "some people don't hate me."
- **Create an experiment** to test this hypothesis. What would you need to do to genuinely put this belief to the test? Perhaps you could look for instances in the past in which people have told you they liked you, or you could observe the behavior of those around you in a period of a week to see how they behave to you—and see whether this is compatible with an attitude of "hate."
- **Run the experiment** as open-mindedly as you can and write down your observations. Perhaps you notice that many people deliberately reach out to you during the week

to ask to spend time with you, and go out of their way to be around you.

- **Analyze these results**. What conclusion can you make? Does the original belief of "everyone hates me" stand up to scrutiny? Notice, also, the change in feeling you have when you change the belief.
- **Make adjustments** to this belief, and when you're unsure, come back to your experiment and remind yourself that you have logically and practically proven to yourself otherwise. Remember the feelings associated with the alternative belief.

There are several different types of behavioral experiments that you can opt for. The one mentioned above is called a "direct hypothesis testing experiment." However, some things that we might overthink about do not lend themselves to forming hypotheses as easily as this method of experimentation. Other times, fears and negative thoughts are not as easy to test. For example, a lonely person who keeps wondering whether anyone would care if something were to happen to them cannot (and should not) test this by, say, harming himself to see if anyone becomes concerned.

For such scenarios, we can employ an alternative experiment method that utilizes surveys. Say you suffer from intrusive thoughts that you believe are so disgusting and embarrassing that you can never share them with another person. The way you can utilize surveys is to either ask people you know who suffer from anxiety about the intrusive thoughts they have, or look for personal accounts online. You'll likely come across many stories of people who have similar thoughts as you, which will normalize your own thoughts and allow you to view them as less harmful or dangerous than you originally perceived.

A third type of behavioral experiment is called discovery experiments. Often, people with anxiety hold on to certain views about specific people, the world in general, and even themselves that are not based on any clearly identifiable reason. However, they have internalized their irrational fears to such an extent that they can't really hypothesize an alternative thought. They're simply convinced if they don't avoid certain things or don't do certain things, the outcome will be bad. For example, a girl who was sexually abused as a child may have come to routinely feel ashamed and somehow "damaged" by her abuser. There isn't a clear reason why being abused would render a person forever damaged, but because she has lived with this experience and thought this way for so long, it might be hard for her to think "maybe I'm not damaged."

In such a case, the person should ask themselves, "What would happen if I acted as if I weren't damaged?" The difference between this type of experiment and hypothesis testing is that you're not merely evaluating the truthfulness of a certain statement or thought. You're enacting it to see how people around you respond to it. Though this can seem daunting, for many this might be the only way of actually finding out whether what they believe is true, because reflection and thinking it through isn't effective. Moreover, of all the types of experiments, you're most likely to be convinced by this one because your own experience will speak for itself.

Create experiments for those stubborn core beliefs you hold. Sometimes, we develop these beliefs because of past experiences and old habits that have become entrenched. Sometimes, the best way to convince yourself of a change is to literally try it out for real. Practical action can kick us out of mental ruts and allow us to *experience* alternatives, rather than just superficially imagine them.

Using CBT to Clean Up Your Self-Talk

In taking a closer look at your thoughts, you might have been overwhelmed by *just how many* thoughts there were—instead of a single idea here and there, overthinkers tend to have a constant, gushing stream of inner dialogue. It can be difficult to pick just a single idea from this constant flow. Self-talk can be defined as the near-constant narrative and commentary we have running mentally as we go about life. It can be neutral (i.e., just noting and observing), positive (i.e., encouraging happy and empowered feelings), or negative (i.e., making us feel awful and, for the purposes of this book, anxious).

What's the difference between a single maladaptive core belief (such as "I have to be perfect to be loved") and negative self-talk? Granted, the concepts overlap significantly. The primary difference can be explained with an example: a core belief of "I have to be perfect to be loved" may result in a whole stream of self-talk and inner narrative, such as: *You're such a loser. Look at how badly this project is turning out. I knew it. Who's going to want to hang around you when you're this useless? Okay, stop feeling sorry for yourself. Nobody wants to be friends with someone who's this neurotic. No wonder you're still single! You fail everything you try, you know? Why is that? I don't even know what's wrong with you . . ."* and so on.

It wouldn't be helpful to address each of these negative statements individually, but with some patience and self-awareness, it can be seen that they all stem from one core belief that expresses itself in different ways. Negative self-talk can be recognized by its emotional character—can you see the shame, self-doubt, and reproach in the self-talk above? It's not so much that this stream of self-talk is inaccurate (although of course it is) but rather that it's . . . well, mean!

CBT can also help us get a handle on the self-talk that comes from chronically low self-esteem, self-judgment, and self-doubt. Using the ABC structure above or the dysfunctional thought record, we can see what triggers our stream of self-talk—which can be difficult at times because it can be so unconscious and so continuous that you don't really know when it "started." But use these records to see if you can distill a single *emotional theme* behind your self-talk, and from that, extract a core belief or thought that sets this train of thought off.

When dealing with chronic, deep-seated self-talk, the healthier alternative is often more emotional than it is cognitive. You might find that instead of dwelling on the accuracy, truth, or logic of the thoughts rushing through your mind, you need to identify the emotion behind it and address that directly. In our example above, this may mean not only changing the thought to, "I am imperfect and lovable just as I am," but looking at the feelings of low self-esteem that come with it and replacing them with self-love and compassion.

Self-Scripting: Fostering and Reinforcing Positive Self-Talk

It's an unavoidable truth that thoughts, feelings, and behavior are always entangled in complex ways. The *language* that we use when we talk to ourselves makes as much of a difference as the factual accuracy of the statements. The way we address ourselves internally is more than just the single thoughts we entertain, but rather an ongoing attitude and habit. Just as we would with any other relationship, we can over time build a relationship with ourselves that is characterized by kindness and respect.

A "self-script" goes beyond individual statements and ideas and extends to having an optimally encouraging and positive way of talking to and about yourself all the time. What voice do you use with yourself? Is it positive or negative? Accurate or inaccurate? Realistic or unrealistic? Kind or unkind? Helpful or unhelpful?

A deliberate self-script is a way to take control of our inner dialogue. If you can engage in a self-script during moments of stress and overthinking, with time it may become more automatic. A self-script can be used when you're doing meditation, visualization, or progressive muscle relaxation, or you can combine it with mantras and encouraging quotes to draw on in tense moments. Create an inspiring self-talk script when you're feeling strong and happy, and return to it when you're anxious or distressed to get you back on track.

If you are familiar with your triggers, you can remind yourself to "switch on" your script when you know you're most vulnerable to delving into negative self-talk or overthinking. For example, knowing that public speaking tends to trigger you, you could work hard to combine breathing techniques, calming visualizations, and inner talk along the lines of, "You've got this. Giving a speech isn't the end of the world, and you've done it well tons of times before . . ." to counter catastrophizing and all-or-nothing distortions. This way you prepare yourself and take charge.

A self-script is a little like self-hypnosis and draws your attention to where you want it. Self-talk may be unconscious, but a deliberate self-script lets you take conscious control. Practice it when you're calm and focused so you are ready and it comes automatically when you're feeling more stressed out. Write it down or post a few key phrases up on your wall where you can see them. After a while, notice the changes in mood and thoughts the script creates (if any) and make tweaks as you go. You can have several different scripts for different situations, triggers, cognitive distortions, or fears.

Your inner cheerleader: the source of a positive self-script.

In working hard to counterbalance any negativity and anxiety you identify in yourself, you may find it helpful to construct the opposite voice: instead of the inner critic, become curious about your inner cheerleader.

This is the voice that wants the very best for you. It's the wisest, highest, and most evolved part of yourself. Whether you think of this as a separate being (a guardian angel, a deity, or a higher power), a mythical or narrative concept (a fairy godmother), or simply a more enlightened and elevated part of yourself, you can consciously choose to have this inner cheerleader weigh in every time you notice any distorted thoughts and core beliefs.

For example, when that negative inner voice chimes in with an anxious criticism or worry, you can deliberately ask your inner cheerleader to respond. Maybe this plays out like a literal dialogue between your self-doubt and your growing confidence.

"You're going to mess this up, I just know it."

"That's not true—you can't know the outcome because it hasn't happened yet. You have many talents and you've worked hard."

"Yes, but there's always a chance that something unlucky happens, and everything goes up in smoke, and then I don't know what I'll do . . ."

"It doesn't matter if it does. You're a lovable, worthwhile individual even if you don't succeed at this the first time. Whatever happens, you're committed to learning, so what is there to be afraid of?"

And so on. Essentially, you are arguing against a knee-jerk negative and anxious bias with a part of you that is committed to your success and wellbeing. If having a little to-and-fro dialogue with yourself feels artificial, just try it—you may be surprised at just how wise and clear-sighted you can be if only you take the opportunity to listen!

A word on "positivity": we all know that phony affirmations and mantras that you don't actually believe won't help much. Positive self-talk doesn't mean being woefully out of touch with reality, lying to yourself, or pretending that problems don't exist. It simply means you're willing to give your perception of life a *slight positive bias*.

Remember that your goal is not to completely eliminate stress, uncertainty, or challenge. You are not putting yourself in a la-la land where everything is perfect. Some stress enhances your performance and can be motivating!

Takeaways

- Many of us are stuck in certain specific negative thought patterns that cause us a lot of anxiety. Cognitive behavioral therapy can help you identify these thought patterns and replace them with more positive attitudes, which will improve your mental health significantly.

- The first thing you need to do is identify the different cognitive distortions you might be falling prey to. Some common ones are black-and-white thinking, wherein you perceive everything in extremes as either horrible or heavenly, and discounting the positives to disproportionally focus on the bad in any given scenario. There is a long list of such distortions, and we likely employ several different ones together.

- Next, we turn our focus to what kind of situations, people, or surroundings trigger specific thought patterns for you. You can use the dysfunctional thought record as a way to keep track of the relevant details. Here, whenever you feel yourself slipping into a negative thought pattern, stop and identify the place, situation, or events that preceded the thought, what exactly the thought was, and which type of distortion it was. Then, think of a rational response to this thought.

- Once we understand more about our cognitive distortions, we need ways to change these thought patterns. One effective way to do this is through behavioral experiments. A simple way to use this technique is to clearly state your negative thought or belief. Then, form a hypothesis wherein you consider the possibility of it being false. Think about whether you have any evidence or past experience that might indicate that the belief is in fact false. Make observations that might point to the same, and if you find reasons to doubt your original belief, analyze them and make changes to your thought pattern accordingly.

Chapter 6. Newfound Attitudes and Emotional Regulation

In this book, we've looked at the problem of overthinking (which is really a problem of anxiety) from a number of different angles and considered solutions ranging from managing time and life stressors, to taking control of your own thoughts and emotions, to reducing the literal tension and stress in your body. We've considered a few scientific models and the research that supports them while acknowledging that applying these findings to our own lives is something of an art.

The goal in all of this is to not just learn a few tips and tricks in the moment (though these are useful), but to become a whole new person—the kind of person who is calm, in control, and faces life with all the confidence of someone who knows their heart and mind and has quiet mastery over both. What is really the difference between a person overwhelmed by negative overthinking and someone who can face any challenge and tension with resilient composure? It's all about attitude.

This chapter collects the spirit of the techniques we've outlined earlier to gather in one place a mindset and perspective that belongs to the non-anxious person. It's a "manifesto" of five thoughts or, more accurately, attitudes. You can always choose to be more aware, and you can always choose *where to direct your awareness*. If you know anyone who is naturally calm in themselves, you might notice that they have one or more of these attitudes running through their own personal narratives. But what they do naturally you can learn to do with a bit of conscious cultivation. The hope is that when practiced regularly, the techniques in previous chapters will naturally lead to these attitudes.

Attitude 1: Focus on what you *can* control, not on what you *can't*

Your conscious awareness can only shine on one thing at a time—so what are you going to focus on? Anxious overthinking occurs when we feel powerless and out of control. When we focus our awareness on those things that are outside our scope of control, we naturally feel powerless. We ignore all the ways we *are* at liberty to make changes, and dwell instead on those things that distress us, without us having any agency to act. It's like we put a spotlight on everything that we can do nothing about and forget about other options and solutions just out of our field of vision. The solutions are there; we just need to turn our attention onto them.

It's like pushing against an immovable stone block—the pushing gets you nowhere and only exhausts and demoralizes you. If it can't be moved, it can't be moved. So why waste energy and attention on it? Why waste effort, especially when that effort could go somewhere else where it has a real chance of making a change!

True, sometimes your scope of action is very limited, and you might only have available to you the choice between two options you don't really like. Still, you have a choice. Often, the only thing you can control is yourself—but that's plenty! For example, you have a minor car accident on the road, due entirely to the negligence of the other driver, who was texting and now denies it and instead wants to yell at you for being an idiot.

It's human to get carried away in fear, anger, or unhappiness in moments like these. But what will getting upset really achieve? Follow the Stoics and gracefully accept what is not in your power to change. Your energy is better spent on quickly getting insurance details and finding ways to get out of the situation as fast as possible so you can get your car repaired. Is the other person wrong? Yes. Are they annoying and stressful and terrible? Probably. But you don't have to pick up that stress. You can refuse to take the bait, ignore their insults, and act in a practical, stress-free manner.

The ancient Stoics understood these principles well, with Epictetus saying, "Just keep in mind: the more we value things outside our control, the less control we have." We have power over our minds, not outside events. So, if we continue to focus on outside events that we don't have power over, the conclusion is obvious—we repeatedly experience powerlessness and therefore anxiety.

In fact, researchers today are discovering evidence that the Stoic principle of focusing on what you can control has measurable benefits for those with anxiety. In 2020, researchers at the Affective and Cognitive Neuroscience Lab at Birkbeck, led by Alexander MacLellan, considered the effect of a Stoic training program on participants. The experimental group succeeded in reducing their rumination by around thirteen percent compared to control groups who didn't do the Stoic training. The exciting part is that the exercises they chose were no different from the ones contained in this book.

Attitude 2: Focus on what you can *do*, not on what you can't

This leads us to the next core attitude. Anxiety and overthinking have a peculiar characteristic—it's all abstract, internal, vague. It's all about possibilities, fears, what-ifs, memories, and conjecture—nothing more substantial than air when you think about it. If you live in your head in this way, you may naturally feel disempowered, as though you were only there to passively witness the world around you and ruminate over it, rather than acknowledging your power to be an active participant. Sometimes, when we're overcome with stressful overthinking, it's because we're afraid to act, or feel like we can't act, or are failing to acknowledge that we can and even should act.

Action has a clarifying and sobering effect and can bring you out of mental conjecture and stressful rumination. If you are not focusing on action, or if you're stressing about what can't be done, you are directing your energy to everything that will make you feel frustrated and useless. We emphasize this feeling of powerlessness and shut our eyes to potential solutions.

Imagine someone who wants to open a bar but discovers with disappointment that red tape and legislature prevent them from acquiring an alcohol license. They're stuck. The entire plan seems to fall apart. So, they start to focus on the fact that they can't do anything, that it's unfair, that it's stumped them . . . and this causes stress.

But a change in perspective could allow them to ask, "If I can't do this, what can I do? Why not open a café instead?"

In an ideal world, we can use our cognitive powers to solve problems, dream up creative solutions, or see a novel way through a strange new situation. Thinking is a precious skill—

provided it inspires action. Action without thinking is idiocy, but thinking without action is anxiety.

The right attitude turns adversity and obstacles into an opportunity for creative solutions. Stress and worry can be channeled into planning and innovation. The best inventors often arrive at amazing ideas precisely *because* their original plans failed. But when you focus on the failure and not the new possibilities suggested by this failure, you place stress on yourself needlessly.

Attitude 3: Focus on what you *have*, not on what you *don't have*

Are you sensing a theme? Confidence and contentment come from a perspective that focuses on possible solutions and positive interpretations, whereas anxiety comes from that perspective that homes in on everything that's wrong with a situation. One is expansive, empowering, and based on curiosity, whereas the other is constricting, disempowering, and based on apathy and foregone conclusions. It's a glass half full, glass half empty kind of thing.

Focusing on what you have is a way to put a positive, healthy spin on your appraisal of any situation. What resources do you have? What's working well? What do you actually have to be grateful for? If you hold this frame of mind, you are primed to see solutions and new opportunities. On the other hand, when you are dwelling on what is missing, what you lack, or what is wrong, that's all you can see. You might completely miss the very solution that would take you out of your unhappiness, were you not focusing on it so intently.

A very simple example: imagine someone is hosting a child's birthday party and has to cater for a huge number of people—quite a stressful feat! Through a minor tragedy, the cake has fallen on the floor and is now completely ruined. The host could stress about this fact and focus on how awful it is that the party is ruined and that there's no cake, or they could see the humor in the situation and get creative in the kitchen. They still have candles, a giant watermelon, party decorations, and mountains of candy. Why not make a game of it and give a prize to the group of children who can dream up the best impromptu birthday cake by the end of the afternoon?

Overthinkers can sometimes blow a problem out of proportion while simultaneously downplaying their own ability to solve it. They make a mountain out of a molehill and then convince themselves there's nothing they can do about it. Even in the face of genuine disaster, calm people have a trust in their own competence and resilience to find a way through.

While we're considering this attitude, it's worth looking at another related concept that has commanded significant research attention in the last few years: gratitude. Being grateful means acknowledging and enjoying everything that is currently going well for you—in a way, the opposite of the stressed and anxious orientation. In 2016, Wong and associates found that "gratitude writing" led to statistically significant increases in mental wellbeing. Patients receiving psychotherapy were divided into three groups: those who wrote "gratitude letters" expressing their thankfulness to others, those who wrote expressively, simply documenting their thoughts and feelings, and those who wrote nothing. As you can guess, the grateful group experienced the biggest boost in wellbeing.

Deliberately turn your mind to focus on the things that are actually *not* problems for you at the moment. We can easily discount those, but simply remaining aware of how blessed we are in so many ways can act as a buffer for all the things we occasionally find challenging.

Attitude 4: Focus on the present, not the past or the future

Anxiety always lives elsewhere. It lingers around in the past, worrying about what has already happened (i.e., is out of your control, see attitude 1), or floats uselessly into the future, imagining a million stressful possibilities. But conscious awareness and useful action don't belong elsewhere: they live in the present. Pull your awareness to what is going on *right now*, and you narrow the scope for overthinking. You also put your thoughts on the one place where they have the best chance of actually helping you. Any solution, any happiness, any insight, and any helpful action is only ever going to be in one place: here. So that's where you should look for it.

To take an example a little more serious than a child's birthday party, think about someone who is struggling with a history of abuse, loss, mental illness, and general dark times. They are at a point in their lives where they are not only distraught about things that have happened and mistakes they have made, but also about what this means for their future and where they're going. Let's say after years of therapy and personal development, this person meets a new romantic partner and things are going brilliantly.

But rather than focus on this budding new romance, they're carried away with regrets about a bad past relationship. They worry that this will threaten their new relationship and that all future connections will be forever tainted by the mistakes and regrets of the past. They keep waiting for "the other shoe to drop" and are so committed to the idea of themselves as a damaged, complicated person that they constantly worry about when everyone else is going to realize what a mess-up they are.

All the while, one thing is overlooked: the fact that *in the present, right now, things are wonderful!* How many people mourn the passing of certain long-gone moments without realizing that this makes it impossible to appreciate the brand-new moment they have right now? How much energy and time is wasted worrying about potential futures that never come—as all the while the real, concrete present moment is dismissed?

Attitude 5: Focus on what you *need*, not what you *want*

There is a simplicity to the non-anxious way of thinking. Our personal inner narratives and our self-talk can weave convoluted worlds that have very little relation to our actual lives. One way we can get sidetracked with stressful overthinking is to misunderstand what is absolutely necessary to our happiness and well-being . . . and what is a nice, optional extra.

Focusing on needs rather than wants helps you get to the core of things and prioritize what's ultimately important. Again, it's always less stressful to focus on what really matters and let go of what doesn't. For example, someone might be planning a big move to a new area and start to feel overwhelmed and stressed out when they think about all the little details of the kind of house that would suit their lifestyle best. They end up getting carried away with ruminations over smaller and smaller details—*Place A has a great garden but is more expensive than Place B, which nevertheless is closer to the shops, but then again, Place C is cheaper and closest to the shops, but has no garden at all . . . But do you care about the garden when it has such amazing wood floors? But then again . . .*

Entertaining endless possibilities and choices may seem smart, but it can actually paralyze you and make your decisions less effective. Trying to endlessly optimize takes us further and further away from our core values and gets us distracted with things that are important but not fundamental. Instead, the person in our example could stop and draw up a list of three main features they need most in a new house. After deciding that price, a garden, and three bathrooms are nonnegotiable, they're able to focus their attention and ignore options that don't measure up.

Focusing on needs also allows you to be more resilient with changes, challenges, or disappointments that aren't great but aren't the end of the world. If we can understand that something is just a want and not a need, it's easier to let go and move on when we don't get it.

Finally, it's worth noting that human beings are often rather bad at guessing what it is they really want and bad at predicting what will make them happy. When you focus on your most basic and fundamental needs, you're forced to think of your truest values; thinking about wants and desires, however, can leave you in murkier water. Who of us hasn't gotten into trouble because we overthought a choice or convinced ourselves about something we were sure we wanted but didn't really?

Practice a bit of mental minimalism, trim things down, and don't try to control big decisions to an extreme degree. We can all get confused by what we think we should want, by what other people want for us, by cultural and social expectations, by advertising, or by any other fleeting whims and whimsies that are less substantial than they seem. True needs are often felt simply and directly, whereas those decisions and desires we notice ourselves endlessly justifying and explaining are usually not genuine needs.

There is another way in which a shift to a focus on needs helps reduce overall anxiety. If you are someone who ruminates on your relationships or finds social stressors make up the bulk of your anxieties, then tuning into needs can help you simplify things. The Nonviolent Communication model proposed by Marshall Rosenberg is about improving empathy, connection, and understanding in relationships. One principle is to focus on needs in social interactions. Take the stress and coercion out of communication by clearly sharing your own needs and listening for the needs of others. This will drastically improve harmony and cut down on relationship distress and anxiety.

As an example, someone may invite themselves over to your house on a day you feel particularly antisocial and not up to seeing anyone. Instead of focusing on their (annoying) actions, going into blame or avoidance, or making excuses that you then feel guilty about, zoom out of that rumination and just look at everyone's respective needs. "Hey, I know you really wanted to hang out tonight, but I need some downtime at the moment. Would it work for you to meet next week instead?" Focusing on needs avoids so many potential avenues of stress.

As you can see, the five attitudes on this manifesto are really variations on a single theme. People who are not subject to anxious overthinking have mastered a particular attitude to life that's characterized by flexibility, focus, resilience, and beneficial action. Put your awareness on everything that is good in any situation—i.e., your options, your resources, your potential for action, and your constant ability to act in your own best interests no matter what adversities you face.

Emotion Regulation via the Opposite Action

The attitudes above shape our thinking, our perception, our behavior, and, ultimately, our world.

Feeding these attitudes is a conscious commitment to positivity, flexibility, hope, gratitude, curiosity, patience, self-respect, and maybe even a little good humor—in other words, the big difference is an *emotional* one. When we can recognize and master our own emotions, we can adopt the emotional state of mind that serves us best. Mastery over self is mastery over body, mind, and heart, or our emotions.

The CBT techniques mentioned above as well as the mindfulness-based methods teach us how to sit with our emotions without judgment. We look in calm awareness at what we feel, accepting our feelings. This is important—emotional regulation begins with emotional acceptance. We do not become better at working with our emotions by learning to push them away, but by learning their names and becoming well acquainted with them.

One technique used with plenty of success in other therapeutic contexts is called the opposite action technique, which, put very crudely, is "doing the opposite of what your emotions tell you." Of course, this doesn't mean denial or fighting against genuine feeling. Indeed, to practice this technique, we need to first dwell on what emotions we really do feel when we overthink (for example, fear, panic, uneasiness, shame) and observe them without resistance or clinging. You've already had a little practice with this when you compiled your CBT or dysfunctional thought record.

This first part of the emotional regulation process is not dissimilar from other meditative practices—you are simply letting your emotions be what they are. With quiet awareness of the breath, your body and your presence, you simply watch yourself and what emotions arise in you. You could pair this inquiry into your emotional state with a scheduled mindfulness practice, add it onto your morning routine, or build it into a visualization session. Or you could practice "being with" yourself and your emotions whenever difficult sensations arise or you feel yourself in a crisis.

There is nothing wrong with having emotions, especially, in the case of overthinking, emotions that are primarily fearful. You have every right and reason to feel as you do. However, we've seen that emotion connects to our thoughts and our behavior. While we feel what we feel, it doesn't mean that we don't have a say over how those feelings affect our thoughts or our behaviors.

The emotion behind much overthinking is fear— fear of being out of control, of being overwhelmed, of failure, of impending danger, of panic, and so on. The feeling is valid. But that doesn't mean it's *true*. It certainly doesn't mean it's helpful! And if we act out of fear, we often only end up creating more fear anyway. But we have the option to observe our feelings, to feel our fear, but to nevertheless *choose* to act differently. This is where the opposite action technique comes in.

If we are stuck in overthinking and anxious rumination, for example, our fearful emotional state could cause a range of different behaviors in us: we might avoid people or situations, fail to take reasonable risks, stop exploring or having curiosity for the world, become suspicious or even paranoid, think less about ourselves and our competencies, scale down our dreams and goals, go into denial about difficult situations, pass up good opportunities for fear of failure, or perhaps blame others for causing our life problems.

The thoughts we have when we are consumed with fear and anxiety are just as limiting:

"The world isn't safe."

"You can't trust anyone."

"It won't work out well; you might as well not even try."

"Don't stick your neck out; it's too risky."

"Don't try anything new; something bad will happen."

We can have compassion for our fearful feelings and validate them as real and painful without necessarily indulging them. In other words, our fearful and anxious emotions are more than welcome to ride with us in the car, but they don't get to be in the driver's seat and decide where our life is going!

What is the opposite of fear and anxiety? What happens when we simply invert these emotions, behaviors, and actions?

We see confidence and relaxation. We approach new situations with interest and aren't afraid to try new things or take a risk. We trust others because deep down, we trust ourselves and know that we are equal to the trials life throws our way and that we can handle them. Sometimes we feel scared, but we allow challenge to motivate and inspire us. Our head is filled with thoughts like, "What happens if I try XYZ?" or, "I don't know what will happen, but I'm hopeful anyway."

In the same way as our CBT spreadsheet allowed us to identify unhealthy thoughts and then think of better alternatives, the opposite action technique enables us to identify the emotional core behind these thoughts so we can try out an alternative that feels better. The general process is:

1. Identify and acknowledge the emotion and experience it without judgment or interpretation
2. Look at the thoughts this emotion is causing you to have, as well as the behaviors it encourages. Do you like these thoughts and behaviors, do they bring you closer to your goals, and are they in line with your values? Are they overpowering or working against you?
3. If so, identify the *opposite* emotion. By trying to cultivate this emotional experience instead, you bring some balance to your state of mind and steer your thoughts and behaviors in a healthier direction.
4. For a fixed period of time (whether it's five minutes or a day), *fully commit* to maintaining the opposite emotional state. If you waver, try

to remember why you're doing the technique at all. Remind yourself of the cost of thoughts and behavior driven by strong negative emotions, as well as the better state of mind you want instead.

5. Observe the results. Notice how you feel compared to at the start, and notice how your thoughts and actions change when you deliberately choose to feel differently. Remember these results the next time you experience a similar strong negative emotion.

This technique is not about denying how you feel or squashing down emotions—quite the opposite! It's a great way to begin to practice better emotional regulation and self-control, bringing consciousness to what is so often an automatic and unhealthy dip into negative thoughts and behavior patterns.

Recall the earlier example of getting in a car accident and having the other driver behave aggressively to you. Rage and anger might dominate. But if you have presence of mind to stop and identify what is going on, you have the chance to change it. Seeing that the thoughts and possible behaviors that come from extreme anger are not likely to be in anyone's best interest, you can deliberately try to pursue the opposite emotion.

Instead of returning anger and insult to the hostile driver, you make the conscious decision that, for the next ten minutes, you are *not* going to get mad, yell, or make accusations. You use a soft voice. You de-escalate, stay neutral, and validate the other driver without necessarily agreeing with him. You notice tension in your neck and choose to let it go. You just have to do this for ten minutes—it's not so bad!

But at the end of ten minutes, once the altercation is over, you might observe a few things: when you look at how you feel now, you realize that that immediate flush of anger isn't really there anymore. You feel relieved you didn't say or do anything you'd be regretting now. And best of all, a sense of *genuine* calm seems to come over you, and you are more quickly able to let go of ruminations about what happened. Whereas you might have stewed over the injustice of it all for hours, now you find it easier to let go and move on.

All of this was achieved without denying the fact that you felt angry or tense. In fact, you could have easily chosen to feel that anger after the ten minutes was up when you felt it was more appropriate. This technique makes full allowance for the fact that these emotions exist—but it doesn't mean that we have to entertain every single one the second it appears, or that we have to let it dictate to us what we think, say, or do. Isn't that an empowering thought?

A Word on Ruminating

What does it mean to ruminate? We've used this word a few times in this book already but never quite defined it in a useful way.

This word actually has a fascinating history: the word originates from the Latin term rūmināre, which literally means to chew over. This is why animals that "chew the cud" such as cows are called "ruminants." It's an apt way to describe a particular kind of thinking we all engage in from time to time. A cow ruminates by regurgitating partially digested material and re-chewing it, usually several times over. Mental rumination is just the same—we regurgitate old memories, ideas, and stale old themes to chew over again and again and again. But whereas chewing a cud is healthy and normal for a cow, rumination is seldom healthy and normal for a human!

Let's say you had a weird disagreement with a loved one and you keep playing the conversation over again in your mind. Maybe you imagine you saying something else, or you're filled with regret or remorse. Something doesn't feel right about it all, so your brain keeps returning to the same scene, dwelling on it, putting a bright spotlight on every ugly detail, trying on different interpretations and hypothetical endings. Basically, rumination is overthinking.

It's chewing ideas down into a pulp, and it's unproductive. Often, we bring out an old memory that in turn triggers other (usually negative) memories, which catches us in a tightening loop of distraction and even more overthinking. You're chewing and chewing, but your problem-solving capacity is only getting worse and your anxiety is rising. In other words, you can't stop telling yourself a really bad fairy tale over and over.

If you're a fan of dredging up bad memories from the past, the first step to stopping is to identify your triggers. Maybe it's going back home and seeing your old room. Maybe it's a certain song or a kind of food or the experience of being assessed. Whatever it is, you need to know what effect it has on you so you can act. The second step is to understand the form your rumination takes. Do you dwell on regret? Resentment? Despair? Do you blame others continually or beat yourself up with guilt?

Next, understand that you need both *awareness* and *distance* from this tired old rerun of a story that may have never even been accurate in the first place. In reading the previous techniques and approaches, this should be familiar to you by now. Psychologically take a step back from this story that seems to just run on its own once triggered. As in all the previous mindfulness exercises, simply observe it unfolding without identifying with it, attaching to it, or resisting it.

One way to gain distance is by **labeling**. Give the story a name. You could think, "Oh, here's *The Saga* again," anytime you recognize yourself being triggered into the same old tale of blame and anger. You can gain distance simply by observing thoughts and feelings, rather than being subsumed by them. So, instead of saying, "I'm useless," say, "I'm feeling useless right now." Instead of saying, "I ruined my chances," say, "I'm remembering a particularly painful memory right now." Put a discrete fence around the sensation, and you put limits on it and begin to understand that it is temporary. After all, how much of what we torment ourselves with is actually based in reality, and how much is simply *stories* we choose to tell ourselves?

It's great if you can put a little humor into it, too. When you can find humor, you can be resilient and somehow bigger than the big scary issue you're facing. Tell yourself, "Oh, here we go. My pity party is coming out in full force this afternoon," and try to find the absurdity in it all, imagining a little mini parade with tiny yet laughable balloons trotting out whenever you remember embarrassing events from your childhood. Poke fun at yourself—at the very least, know that you're definitely not the only one to harp on a bad memory.

Another thing to try is to deliberately ask yourself: **is what you're doing problem solving or rumination?** Be honest. On first chew, an idea might actually yield something useful or insightful. But generally, the more you go over an idea, the less you gain from it. We've seen that a powerful antidote to getting stuck in analysis mode is simply to act. Bring yourself into the concrete moment by actually *doing* something, rather than endlessly juggling potentials and guesses and worries.

If the answer is "I'm just ruminating," then force yourself to direct your attention to a single small action right now in the moment. Let's say you messed up and said something mean to a friend without thinking. You feel bad now. You replay the phrase in your head, cringing each time. Then you stop and ask, "Is what I'm doing problem solving or rumination?" You realize you're just chewing the psychological cud and tell yourself to stop and instead think of a tiny thing you can do to improve the situation.

The problem is that you've offended your friend. The solution could be to apologize or reach out to mend the bridge. So do that. Think of it this way, if you're going to spend all the energy thinking over the problem, at least put it to good use and find a way to improve things. If you can't improve anything, then put your energy into distraction, forgiveness, or moving on.

By rechanneling anxious energy into things that will either improve your situation or at least help you come to terms with it, you are re-engaging with the world and getting out of the endless mental hurricane that goes nowhere but round and round in circles.

We've already spoken about distress tolerance, but you can go a long way to being mentally resilient simply by learning to distract yourself at the right moments. When you notice yourself ruminating ("Ah, here comes my rumination again. It's so boring with its same old stories . . ."), quickly throw yourself into an activity that absorbs all your attention. Get up and do thirty jumping jacks while saying the alphabet backward. Write out your shopping list for the week. Pick up your knitting, tidy your desk, or sing a complicated song, focusing intently on the lyrics. It doesn't really matter what you do, only that you temporarily break the rumination cycle by distracting yourself.

If you can't think of anything, focus on sensations from your five senses, or simply engage in physical activity, such as jogging or yoga. You don't have to stoically sit there and fight off intrusive thoughts—get up and literally shake them off if you like. If you hear your brain dipping into those "would have, should have, could have, what if, maybe" style thoughts, jump in and nip it in the bud. Usually, we want to avoid getting distracted, but distraction can be a powerful tool if we use it consciously and with purpose.

Are you stewing over something you have zero control over?

Are you making a mountain out of a molehill?

Is your rumination doing anything at all to advance the situation or fix the problem?

Do you have any reason to believe that the story you're telling or your interpretation of events is all that great—i.e., should you even take your word for it?

Gain psychological distance by imagining that your rumination is a boring old friend who's always rabbiting on about something. Picture yourself in the position of a calm, impartial observer who knows deep down that the story is just that—a story. So, the boring old friend comes to you and says, "Remember that time a few years ago when you said you knew how to speak French and then someone spoke French to you and you had no idea how to respond? Remember that? That was so humiliating, right?"

Maybe you were triggered into this memory by seeing something on a TV show or recently met a friend who was there when the incident happened. In whatever way the rumination was triggered, though, once you are aware of it, you have two choices. You can join in with the friend and have a good, long, angsty discussion about how cringe-worthy the whole episode was and how much you suck as a person for telling such a stupid lie. *Or*, you could calmly tell the rumination, "Ah, yes, I know this old yarn. But that's in the past now. I learned my lesson and don't do that kind of thing to big myself up anymore, and people have long since forgotten my gaffe. Now, let me return to what I was doing . . ."

When the boring rumination friend pipes up again and invites you to replay the embarrassing scene, you respond with, "Hey, rumination, do you have anything new to say? Do you have any fresh ideas for practical steps I can take right now? If not, then goodbye. I'm busy with something else." Your mind is like Teflon. Easy. The rumination, a little disappointed that nobody is listening, wanders off.

Takeaways

- Though this book lays down a ton of strategies to help you cope with anxiety and overthinking, the goal here isn't just to learn some tips and tricks. It's to have a more transformational impact by inducing a fundamental change in our attitudes and perceptions. There are five such attitudes which you need to incorporate into your mindset.
- The first is to focus on what you can control and not on what you can't. If you can control something, do it. But if you can't, there's no use worrying about it. In the end, there's nothing you can do, and the best strategy here

is to simply accept that and move on. The second is to focus on what you can do, and not on what you can't. This is similar to the first, but more specific. What are specific things you can and can't do in certain situations?

- The third attitude is to concentrate on what you have, and not on what you don't. We often forget to appreciate all the good things we have at our disposal while focusing overwhelmingly on what's missing. However, we can correct this by consciously thinking of the good things in our life. Similarly, hone in on what you need and not what you want, because the things you want will never end and will never be entirely achievable. This will help you focus on things that are absolutely necessary. Lastly, live in the present, not the past or the future, because what ifs are the best way to fall prey to overthinking.

- Rumination is anxious, unproductive overthinking. Like other types of anxiety, it can be addressed with awareness and psychological distance. Label thoughts as thoughts and personify or externalize old stories and get into the habit of asking whether what you're doing is genuine problem solving or just rumination.

CHAPTER 1. OVERTHINKING ISN'T ABOUT OVERTHINKING

- What exactly is overthinking? Overthinking is when you excessively analyze, evaluate, ruminate, and worry about certain things to a point where it starts affecting your mental health because you simply can't stop.
- There are two main sources of anxiety which lead to overthinking. The first one is ourselves. Unfortunately, some of us are just genetically predisposed to being more anxious than others. However, genetics may not be the only factor. We might become habitual overthinkers because it makes us feel like we're somehow tackling the problem we're overthinking about. Because the overthinking never ends, this doesn't happen, but we still feel like we're making some progress. This turns into a vicious cycle that can be hard to escape.

- Another cause of anxiety is our environment. There are two aspects to this. First, we need to consider our immediate environments where we spend the most time, like our home and office. The way these spaces have been designed can have a huge impact on our anxiety levels. If they're cluttered, dimly lit and noisy, it's going to make us more anxious. The second aspect is the broader experience we have in our socio-cultural setting through our interactions with the world. Something like experiencing racism or sexism might make us stressed and result in heightened anxiety.
- There are many negative consequences to overthinking. These include physical, mental, and even social harms that can become long-term issues. Some examples are racing heart, dizziness, feelings of fatigue, irritability, nervousness, headaches, muscle tension, etc.

CHAPTER 2. THE DE-STRESS FORMULA AND THEN SOME

- Now that we've identified what overthinking is, we need to know how to combat it. There are many things you can do to de-stress and calm an anxious, overthinking mind that are simple, yet effective.

- The first thing you need to remember is a mantra called the 4 As of stress management. These are avoid, alter, accept, and adapt. Avoiding things entails simply walking away from things you can't control. Some things are simply not worth the effort and are best removed from our environments altogether. However, if we can't avoid it, we must learn how to alter our environment to remove the stressor. If we can't alter our environment, we have no choice but to accept it. Lastly, if we can't do much about the situation at all, we must adapt to it and learn how to cope with our stressor and reduce its damaging potential to a minimum.
- Another popular technique is journaling. When we overthink, we have tons of different thoughts swirling in our mind, which can feel overwhelming. However, when we write these down systematically, we can analyze them and evaluate whether these thoughts are merited at all. To build the habit, you can carry a pocket journal with you around and write whenever you feel it's necessary.
- A third technique we have is called the 5-4-3-2-1 technique. This is highly effective at stemming panic attacks, and it does so by involving all five of our senses. So, whenever you feel panic overcoming you, look for five things around you that you can see, four things you can touch, three that you can smell, two that you can hear, and one that you can

taste. Engaging your senses distracts your brain from the overthinking.

CHAPTER 3. MANAGE YOUR TIME AND INPUTS

- One of the biggest sources of our anxiety is poor time management. We tend to prioritize things that make us miserable and refuse to give enough time to things we really enjoy. We seldom take time out for adequate leisure and relaxation, so we must consciously do this in order to improve our anxiety levels. Some tips to follow are making regular to-do lists, prioritizing your tasks in the order of your actual preference, and breaking goals down into smaller pieces.

- There are also other strategies that can help us manage our time better. One of these is called Allen's input processing method. Here, inputs are any external stimulus. What we need to do is analyze and take note of how we respond to even the most minute stimulus, like calls, emails, etc. Then, we must plan for the best way to respond based on our existing responses so that we can prioritize certain stimuli over others.

- Another useful technique is to use SMART goals. This stands for specific, measurable, attainable, relevant, time-bound goals. Note your goals down in very specific detail so you know exactly what to do. Then, set up criteria for measuring how you'll know you've achieved this goal. Make sure that the goal is attainable; it shouldn't be something outlandish. Assess how this goal is relevant to your value system and what purpose achieving it will fulfill in your life. Lastly, set a time limit for completing this goal so that you do it in a reasonable amount of time.

CHAPTER 4. HOW TO FIND INSTANT ZEN

- There may be times where you feel that your anxiety is reaching a fever pitch or that it's on the verge of spiralling out of your control. In such cases, you can rely on some tried and tested techniques to reduce your stress levels.
- The first of these techniques is autogenic training. Through this, we aim to gain control over our thoughts and emotions through six different exercises. To practice the first technique, find a comfortable place to sit or lie down. Then, give yourself certain verbal cues like "I am completely calm" while breathing slowly and steadily. Feel the sensations in

various parts of your body as you intermittently repeat the phrase to yourself. Though this technique might take some time to master, it's simple and can be done anywhere, anytime.

- The second technique is called guided imagery. Essentially, you find a comfortable position and think of a place which engages all your different senses like smell, sound, etc., in pleasantly stimulating ways. This can be any place, it just needs to be one that inspires relaxation. Picture it in as much detail as you can by making full use of your imagination.

- Thirdly, we have progressive muscle relaxation. This technique relies on the theory that physical relaxation leads to mental relaxation. So, the goal is to physically relax your muscles by first tensing them up. Again, sit in a comfortable position and go from head to toe or vice versa and tense different parts of your body before relaxing and moving on.

- Finally, worry postponement is a very direct and effective way of interrupting anxiety spirals. When you recognize yourself beginning to feel anxious, deliberately schedule a discrete time in the future to worry instead, and then continually bring your mind to the present. We can seldom eliminate worry from our lives, but we *can* consciously limit its time of onset and the duration.

CHAPTER 5. REWIRE YOUR THOUGHT PATTERNS

- Many of us are stuck is certain specific negative thought patterns that cause us a lot of anxiety. Cognitive behavioral therapy can help you identify these thought patterns and replace them with more positive attitudes which will improve your mental health significantly.

- The first thing you need to do is identify the different cognitive distortions you might be falling prey to. Some common ones are black and white thinking, wherein you perceive everything in extremes, as either horrible or heavenly, and discounting the positives to disproportionally focus on the bad in any given scenario. There is a long list of such distortions, and we likely employ several different ones together.

- Next, we turn our focus to what kind of situations, people or surroundings trigger specific thought patterns for you. You can use the dysfunctional thought record as a way to keep track of the relevant details. Here, whenever you feel yourself slipping into a negative thought pattern, stop and identify the place, the situation or events that preceded the thought, what exactly the thought was, and which type of distortion it was. Then, think of a rational response to this thought.

- Once we understand more about our cognitive distortions, we need ways to change these thought patterns. One effective way to do this is through behavioral experiments. A simple way to use this technique is to clearly state your negative thought or belief. Then, form a hypothesis wherein you consider the possibility of it being false. Think about whether you have any evidence or past experience which might indicate that the belief is in fact false. Make observations that might point to the same, and if you find reasons to doubt your original belief, analyze them and make changes to your thought pattern accordingly.

CHAPTER 6. NEWFOUND ATTITUDES AND EMOTIONAL REGULATION

- Though this book lays down a ton of strategies to help you cope with anxiety and overthinking, the goal here isn't just to learn some tips and tricks. It's to have a more transformational impact by inducing a fundamental change in our attitudes and perceptions. There are five such attitudes which you need to incorporate into your mindset.

- The first is to focus on what you can control and not on what you can't. If you can control something, do it. But if you can't, there's no use worrying about it. In the end, there's nothing you can do and the best strategy here is to simply accept that and move on. The second is to focus on what you can do, and not on what you can't. This is similar to the first, but more specific. What are specific things you can and can't do in certain situations?

- The third attitude is to concentrate on what you have, and not on what you don't. We often forget to appreciate all the good things we have at our disposal while focusing overwhelmingly on what's missing. However, we can correct this by consciously thinking of the good things in our life. Similarly, home in on what you need and not what you want, because the things you want will never end and will never be entirely achievable. This will help you focus on things that are absolutely necessary. Lastly, live in the present, not the past or the future, because what ifs are the best way to fall prey to overthinking.

- Rumination is anxious, unproductive overthinking. Like other types of anxiety, it can be addressed with awareness and psychological distance. Label thoughts as thoughts and personify or externalize old stories, and get into the habit of asking whether what you're doing is genuine problem solving or just rumination.